Oxford AQA GCSE History (9-1)

Germany 1890-1945

Democracy and Dictatorship

Revision Guide

 RECAP   APPLY   REVIEW   SUCCEED

AUTHOR & SERIES EDITOR
Aaron Wilkes

OXFORD

Great Clarendon Street, Oxford, OX2 6DP, United Kingdom

Oxford University Press is a department of the University of Oxford.

It furthers the University's objective of excellence in research, scholarship, and education by publishing worldwide. Oxford is a registered trade mark of Oxford University Press in the UK and in certain other countries.

British Library Cataloguing in Publication Data

Data available

978-0-19-842289-1

Kindle edition 978-0-19-842290-7

3 5 7 9 10 8 6 4 2

Paper used in the production of this book is a natural, recyclable product made from wood grown in sustainable forests.

The manufacturing process conforms to the environmental regulations of the country of origin.

Printed in Italy by L.E.G.O. S.p.A.

Acknowledgements

The publisher would like to thank Jon Cloake for his work on the Student Book on which this Revision Guide is based and David Rawlings for reviewing this Revision Guide.

We are grateful for permission to include extracts from the following copyright material:

Richard Holmes: *The World At War: the landmark Oral History from the classic TV Series* (Ebury Press, 2007), text copyright © Richard Holmes 2007, used by permission of The Random House Group Ltd.

Eric A Johnson and **Karl-Heinz Reuband**: *What We Knew: Terror, mass-murder, and everyday life in Nazi Germany* (John Murray, 2005), used with the agreement of John Murray Press, an imprint of Hodder & Stoughton.

Lawrence Rees: *The Nazis: A Warning from History* (BBC Books/ Ebury, 2006), copyright © 1997, used by permission of The Random House Group Ltd.

Hjalmar Schacht: *Account Settled* translated by Edward Fitzgerald (Weidenfeld & Nicolson, 1949), used with the agreement of John Murray Press, an imprint of Hodder & Stoughton.

William L. Shirer: *The Rise and Fall of The Third Reich: a history of Nazi Germany* (Arrow books, 1998), copyright © William L Shirer 1960, © renewed 1988 by William L Shirer, used by permission of The Random House Group Ltd and Abner Stein in association with Don Congdon Associates Inc.

We have made every effort to trace and contact all copyright holders before publication. If notified of any errors or omissions, the publisher will be happy to rectify these at the earliest opportunity.

Links to third party websites are provided by Oxford in good faith and for information only. Oxford disclaims any responsibility for the materials contained in any third party website referenced in this work.

Contents

Introduction to this Revision Guide 5

Top revision tips 6

Master your exam skills 7

How to master the 'interpretation questions' 8

How to master the 'describe' question 8

How to master the 'in what ways' question 9

How to master the 'bullet points' question 9

AQA GCSE mark schemes 10

Germany 1890–1945 Timeline 11

Part one:
Germany and the growth of democracy

			RECAP	APPLY	REVIEW

1 Kaiser Wilhelm II and the difficulties of ruling Germany — 12

Parliamentary government, Industrialisation, Growth of socialism 12

Navy Laws. 13

2 Impact of the First World War — 14

Defeat and the end of the monarchy 14

The main political parties in early Weimar Germany. 16

How did the Germans react to the Treaty of Versailles? 17

Impact of economic problems 18

3 Weimar democracy — 20

Political change and unrest, 1919–23 20

The Stresemann era (1924–29), Weimar culture in the 1920s 22

Part two:
Germany and the Depression

4 The impact of the Depression — 24

What was the Depression? 24

Reasons for the growth of the Nazi Party. 25

Reasons for the growth of the Nazi Party (continued) 26

5 The failure of Weimar democracy — 28

Hitler's road to power 28

Contents

6 The establishment of Hitler's dictatorship   30

Elimination of political opposition 30

The Night of the Long Knives 32

Part three:
The experiences of Germans under the Nazis

7 Economic changes in Nazi Germany   34

Back to work.. 34

Self-sufficiency 36

Impact of war 38

8 Social policy and practice in Nazi Germany   40

The Nazis and young people, Hitler Youth Organisation 40

Women in Nazi Germany.. 42

Nazi control of churches and religion 44

Racial policy, persecution and the Final Solution........................ 46

Fighting back: Jewish resistance 47

9 Control in Nazi Germany   48

The police state 48

Propaganda and censorship 50

Art and culture in Nazi Germany....................................... 52

Resistance and opposition... 54

Exam Practice: GCSE sample answers 56

Activity answers guidance 64

Glossary... 70

RECAP   APPLY   REVIEW

Introduction

The *Oxford AQA GCSE History* textbook series has been developed by an expert team led by Jon Cloake and Aaron Wilkes. This matching revision guide offers you step-by-step strategies to master your AQA Period Study: Germany exam skills, and the structured revision approach of **Recap, Apply and Review** to prepare you for exam success.

Use the **Checklists** on pages 3–4 to keep track of your revision, and use the traffic light feature on each page to monitor your confidence level on each topic. Other exam practice and revision features include **Top Revision Tips** on page 6, and the **'How to...'** guides for each exam question type on pages 7–9.

RECAP Each chapter recaps key events and developments through easy-to-digest chunks and visual diagrams. **Key terms** appear in bold and red font; they are defined in the glossary. indicates the relevant Oxford AQA History Student Book pages so you can easily reread the textbook for further revision.

SUMMARY highlights the most important facts at the end of each chapter.

 TIMELINE provides a short list of dates to help you remember key events.

APPLY Each revision activity is designed to help drill your understanding of facts, and then progress towards applying your knowledge to exam questions.

These targeted revision activities are written specifically for this guide, which will help you apply your knowledge towards the six exam questions in your AQA Germany exam paper:

INTERPRETATION ANALYSIS **DESCRIBE** **IN WHAT WAYS** **BULLET POINTS**

 Examiner Tip highlights key parts of an exam question, and gives you hints on how to avoid common mistakes in exams.

 Revision Skills provides different revision techniques. Research shows that using a variety of revision styles can help cement your revision.

 Review gives you helpful reminders about how to check your answers and how to revise further.

REVIEW Throughout each chapter, you can review and reflect on the work you have done, and find advice on how to further refresh your knowledge.

You can tick off the Review column from the progress checklist as you work through this revision guide. **Activity Answers Guidance** and the **Exam Practice** sections with full sample student answers also help you to review your own work.

Top revision tips

Getting your revision right

It is perfectly natural to feel anxious when exam time approaches. The best way to keep on top of the stress is to be organised!

3 months to go

Plan: create a realistic revision timetable, and stick to it!

Track your progress: use the Progress Checklists (pages 3–4) to help you track your revision. It will help you stick to your revision plan.

Be realistic: revise in regular, small chunks, of around 30 minutes. Reward yourself with 10 minute breaks – you will be amazed how much more you'll remember.

Positive thinking: motivate yourself by turning your negative thoughts to positive ones. Instead of asking *'why can't I remember this topic at all?'* ask yourself *'what different techniques can I try to improve my memory?'*

Organise: make sure you have everything you need – your revision books, coloured pens, index cards, sticky notes, paper, etc. Find a quiet place where you are comfortable. Divide your notes into sections that are easy to use.

Timeline: create a timeline with colour-coded sticky notes, to make sure you remember important dates relating to the three parts of the Germany period study (use the Timeline on page 11 as a starting point).

Practise: ask your teachers for practice questions or past papers.

Revision techniques

Using a variety of revision techniques can help you remember information, so try out different methods:

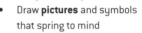

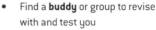
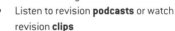

- Make **flashcards**, using both sides of the card to test yourself on key figures, dates, and definitions
- **Colour-code** your notebooks
- **Reread** your textbook or copy out your notes
- Create **mind-maps** for complicated topics
- Draw **pictures** and symbols that spring to mind
- Group study
- Find a **buddy** or group to revise with and test you
- Listen to revision **podcasts** or watch revision **clips**
- Watch revision **clips**
- Work through the **revision activities** in this guide.

Revision tips to help you pass your Germany exam

---

1 month to go

Key concepts: make sure you understand key concepts for this topic, such as democracy, reparations, dictatorship, and propaganda. If you're unsure, attend revision sessions and ask your teacher.

Identify your weaknesses: which topics or question types are easier and which are more challenging for you? Schedule more time to revise the challenging topics or question types.

Make it stick: find memorable ways to remember chronology, using fun rhymes, or doodles, for example.

Take a break: do something completely different during breaks – listen to music, take a short walk, make a cup of tea, for example.

Check your answers: answer the exam questions in this guide, *then* check the Activity answers guidance at the end of the guide to practise applying your knowledge to exam questions.

Understand your mark scheme: review the Mark scheme (page 10) for each exam question, and make sure you understand how you will be marked.

Master your exam skills: study and remember the How to master your exam skills steps (pages 7–9) for each AQA question type – it will help you plan your answers quickly!

Time yourself: practise making plans and answering exam questions within the recommended time limits.

Take mock exams seriously: you can learn from them how to manage your time better under exam conditions.

Rest well: make sure your phone and laptop are put away at least an hour before bed. This will help you rest better.

On the big day

Sleep early: Don't work through the night, get a good night's sleep.

Be prepared: Make sure you know where and when the exam is, and leave plenty of time to get there.

Check: make sure you have all your equipment in advance, including spare pens!

Drink and eat healthily: avoid too much caffeine or junk food. Water is best – if you are 5% dehydrated, then your concentration drops 20%.

Stay focused: don't listen to people who might try to wind you up about what might come up in the exam – they don't know any more than you.

Good luck!

Master your exam skills

Get to grips with your Paper 1: Germany Period Study

The Paper 1 exam lasts 1 hour 45 minutes, and you have to answer 10 questions covering two topics. The first six questions (worth 40 marks) will cover Germany; the last four questions (44 marks) will cover your Conflict and Tension topic. Here, you will find details about what to expect from the first six questions relating to Germany, and advice on how to master your exam skills.

You should spend about 50 minutes in total on the Germany questions – see pages 8–9 for how long to spend on each question. **The six questions will always follow this pattern:**

▼ INTERPRETATION A

_____

_____

▼ INTERPRETATION B

_____

_____

01   How does **Interpretation B** differ from **Interpretation A** about…? Explain your answer using **Interpretations A** and **B.**   [4 marks]

02   Why might the authors of **Interpretations A** and **B** have a different interpretation about …? Explain your answer using **Interpretations A** and **B** and your contextual knowledge.   [4 marks]

03   Which interpretation do you find more convincing about …? Explain your answers using **Interpretations A** and **B** and your contextual knowledge.   [8 marks]

04   Describe two…   [4 marks]

05   In what ways… Explain your answer.   [8 marks]

06   Which of the following was the more important reason…

☐ _____

☐ _____?

Explain your answer with reference to both bullet points.   [12 marks]

REVIEW

If you find interpretations challenging, look out for the INTERPRETATION ANALYSIS activities throughout this guide to help you revise and drill your understanding of the interpretation questions. Look out for the REVISION SKILLS tips too, to inspire you to find the revision strategies that work for you!

REVISION SKILLS

Read the _Conflict and Tension Revision Guide_ for help on the last four questions of Paper 1.

EXAMINER TIP

The **caption** for the interpretations is key. It gives you the provenance, which are the details about when or where it was written or said, and the author's background.

EXAMINER TIP

The actual **content** of the interpretations is equally important – you need to read it carefully and consider the reasons why the author might have written/said it, who they were trying to communicate to, and the tone. Don't just think about what it says, think about _how_ it is said!

EXAMINER TIP

Question 6 will always have two bullet points referring to factors or events. You need to show you can evaluate by deciding which of the bullet points to argue for. This question is worth 12 marks, so make sure you give yourself enough time to plan and write your essay.

How to master the 'interpretation' questions

Here are the steps to consider when answering the three interpretation questions. Remember that each question targets a different aspect of the interpretations.

Question 1

- **Content:** Read the question and the two interpretations carefully, and analyse the contents of both interpretations. What is different in the interpretations? Where does the content differ? Write at least 2–3 differences down. Make sure you refer to both **Interpretations A** and **B**.

- Spend about 5 minutes answering this 4-mark question.

Question 2

- **Context:** This question is about the circumstances in which the interpretations were said/written. What situation was the person in that made them say what they said? Make sure you use the captions (provenances) of each interpretation to help you answer this question.

- Spend about 5 minutes on this 4-mark question.

Question 3

- **Comment:** First, what historical facts can you use to support or challenge each author's view? Use the knowledge you have based on what you've studied about this topic. Again, make sure you comment on both interpretations in turn.

- **Conclude:** Finally, comment on which you find most convincing – which interpretation fits better with what you know about the history of this topic? Your conclusion on which is most convincing should be based on the history that happened, not on who the author is.

- Spend about 10 minutes on this 8-mark question.

How to master the 'describe' question

Here are the steps to consider when answering the 'describe' question.

Question 4

- **Two features:** You have to show what you know and understand about two key features or issues of this period. Make sure you name the two features, then write some historical facts about each of those features.

- Spend about 5 minutes on this 4-mark question.

How to master the 'in what ways' question

Here are the steps to consider when answering the 'in what ways' question.

Question 5

- **What changed and what caused the changes:** You have to explain how a particular group of people experienced changes due to events or government decisions. What were the causes of the changes, and what were the results? Name 2–3 changes, causes, or consequences, then write some facts about each change/cause/consequence.

- Spend about 10 minutes on this 8-mark question.

How to master the 'bullet points' question

The last question on Germany in Paper 1 will always relate to two bullet points. You have to compare the two things named in the bullet points, and come up with a judgement (conclusion) about which is more important. Here are the steps to consider:

Question 6

- **Read the question carefully:** What topic is the question asking about? The topic is located before the colon. Underline the topic and the dates to help you focus your answer.

- **Plan your essay:** Ask yourself, 'what are the historical facts or concepts I know about how each bullet point affected the topic?' Spend 1–2 minutes drawing a quick mind-map to establish your main arguments/historical evidence on each of the bullet points. Try to structure your essay answer in four paragraphs, starting with an introduction, two main paragraphs, and a conclusion.

- **Introduce your argument:** Make sure you name the key topic and dates, and the two bullet points.

- **Analyse each bullet:** For each bullet point, write at least one paragraph about why that point may be more important, or what the impact of the bullet point was.

- **Conclude your argument:** It is important to come to a conclusion. Decide (judge) which bullet point you think was more important, and summarise your argument.

- Spend about 15 minutes on this 12-mark question.

REVIEW

You can find sample student answers to each question type in the **Exam Practice** pages at the end of this guide.

EXAMINER TIP

Don't forget you will have to answer four more questions relating to your Conflict and Tension topic in Paper 1. Ensure you leave enough time to complete both sections of Paper 1! You are advised to spend 50 minutes on your Conflict and Tension topic in the exam.

AQA GCSE History mark schemes

Below are simplified versions of the AQA mark schemes, to help you understand the marking criteria for your **Paper 1: Germany** exam.

Level	Interpretation question 1
2	• Developed analysis of the two interpretations. • Differences are explained with relevant facts. 3–4 marks
1	• Simple analysis of one or two interpretations. • Differences are named. 1–2 marks

Level	Interpretation question 2
2	• Developed analysis of the provenance of the two interpretations. • Differences in the provenance (e.g. time of writing, place, circumstances, audience) are explained with relevant facts/understanding. 3–4 marks
1	• Simple analysis of the provenance of the interpretation(s). • Differences in the provenance (e.g. time of writing, place, circumstances, audience) are named. 1–2 marks

Level	Interpretation question 3
4	• Complex evaluation of the two interpretations. • Argument about which interpretation is more/less convincing is shown throughout the answer, supported by relevant facts/understanding. 7–8 marks
3	• Developed evaluation of the two interpretations. • Argument is stated about which interpretation is more/less convincing. Answer is supported by relevant facts/understanding. 5–6 marks
2	• Simple answer of one interpretation (there may be a basic analysis of the other interpretation). • Answer is supported with relevant facts/understanding. 3–4 marks
1	• Basic answer on one or two interpretations. • Some facts/understanding are shown. 1–2 marks

Level	Describe question
2	• Answer explains relevant facts and understanding. 3–4 marks
1	• Answer names some relevant facts. 1–2 marks

Level	In what ways question
4	• Complex explanation of two or more changes. • A range of accurate, detailed and relevant facts are shown. 7–8 marks
3	• Developed explanation of two or more changes/consequences. • A range of accurate, relevant facts are shown. 5–6 marks
2	• Simple explanation of one change. • Specific relevant facts are shown. 3–4 marks
1	• Basic explanation of change(s). • Some basic related facts are shown. 1–2 marks

Level	Bullet points question
4	• Complex explanation of two bullet points. • A range of accurate and detailed facts that are relevant to the question. 10–12 marks
3	• Developed explanation of two bullet points. • A range of accurate facts shown that are relevant to the question. 7–9 marks
2	• Simple explanation of one or two bullet points. • Specific facts shown that are relevant to the question. 4–6 marks
1	• Basic explanation of one or two bullet points. • Some basic facts shown that are relevant to the question. 1–3 marks

Germany 1890–1945 Timeline

The colours represent different types of event as follows:

 Blue: economic events   Red: political events

 Black: international events or foreign policy   Yellow: social events

1888 Kaiser Wilhelm II becomes Emperor of Germany

1898 Naval race: Germany begins to expand its navy to compete with Britain's navy

1914 First World War begins

1918 **November** – Kaiser Wilhelm II abdicates

November – First World War ends

1919 **January** – Spartacus League revolt

June – Treaty of Versailles is signed

August – Weimar Constitution is established

1920 **January** – American jazz music comes to Germany

February – Founding of the Nazi Party

March – Kapp Putsch

1922 **March** – Foundation of Hitler Youth

1923 **January** – French and Belgian troops invade German industrial area of the Ruhr

Hyperinflation makes money worthless

November – Munich Putsch

1924 Gustav Stresemann becomes Foreign Minister

August – Dawes Plan: US loans money to Germany

1925 **February** – Hindenburg becomes President

1926 **January** – Germany joins League of Nations

1929 **February** – Young Plan is proposed

October – Wall Street Crash, leading to the Great Depression

1930 The Depression takes hold in Germany

1933 Hitler is named Chancellor; after Hindenburg's death in 1934, Hitler becomes Germany's dictator

1934 **June** – Night of the Long Knives; Rohm is arrested and later shot

1936 **August** – Summer Olympics held in Berlin

Membership of the League of German Girls becomes compulsory

1937 Volkswagen car company is formed

1938 **November** – Kristallnacht: Jewish homes, businesses and synagogues attacked

1939 **September** – Germany invades Poland: the Second World War begins

1942 **January** – Wannsee Conference: plan created for extermination of Europe's Jews

Death camps are set up in German-occupied areas

1945 **April** – Hitler commits suicide

May – Surrender of Germany to Allies in the Second World War

CHAPTER 1

Kaiser Wilhelm II and the difficulties of ruling Germany

When Germany was unified as a nation in 1871, the king of the most powerful state, Prussia, became its new ruler, or **Kaiser**.

Parliamentary government

> ▼ **Kaiser: ruled over all the states of Germany.**
>
> **Chancellor** (chief minister) and ministers advised Kaiser.
>
> **Bundesrat**: made up of representatives from each state.
>
> **Reichstag**: parliament elected by men over 25.
>
> Both debated and voted on laws drawn up by the Kaiser and ministers.
>
> **Kaiser**: could ignore government advice and make his own decisions. He made all military and foreign policy decisions.

Kaiser Wilhelm II

- Spent most of his youth in the army
- Keen to maintain a powerful army and build up a large navy
- Took great pride in leading the army and was very interested in military tactics
- Was from **Prussia**; **militarism** – the belief that a country should have strong armed forces – was important to Prussia; Prussian generals, army officers and tactics formed the basis of the new united German army
- Wanted Germany to be a **global power** and have an empire to rival Britain's; this idea was called *Weltpolitik* – 'world policy'

Industrialisation

In the late 1800s, Germany began to **industrialise**. Supported by powerful German businessmen, production of iron and coal doubled. By 1913, Germany was producing as much coal as Britain and more iron and steel. By 1914, Germany produced two-thirds of Europe's steel. In industries such as electrical goods and chemicals, German companies dominated Europe. Some leading factory and business owners had become very rich and influential.

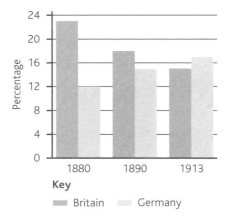

Key
- ▮ Britain
- ▮ Germany

Percentage share of world industrial production

Growth of socialism

> Many workers were unhappy with low wages and poor working conditions.

> Workers joined **trade unions** and **organised strikes** hoping to force the government to improve pay and working conditions. By 1914 over three million workers had joined trade unions.

> A new political party – the **Social Democratic Party (SPD)** – became popular among the workers.
>
> - It believed in **socialism** – power and wealth should be shared equally among the people.
> - It hoped that the Kaiser might allow the Reichstag to make more social reforms or laws to improve workers' rights and conditions.
> - It disagreed with the power and privileged positions held by land and factory owners.
> - Around one in three Germans voted for this political party at this time.

> Some socialists took a more **extreme** view: they wanted to rebel against the Kaiser's rule, start a revolution and allow cities and towns to be governed by councils of workers.

Navy laws

What?

Between 1898 and 1912 a series of **Navy Laws** were introduced. As a result, a huge amount of money was spent to rapidly increase the size of the navy. The army expanded in size too.

Why?

The Kaiser wanted a large navy to help him take over more countries and protect those already in the German Empire.

How?

Taxes were increased and money was borrowed to pay for this. Germany would remain in debt for a very long time.

SUMMARY

- Germany's Kaiser was extremely powerful and could make his own decisions.
- From the late 1800s, Germany's economy expanded as it industrialised. By 1914 it was a world economic power.
- Germany's working class grew as Germany industrialised, but their pay and conditions were poor.
- The new Social Democratic Party (SPD) became popular with workers. It wanted social reforms to improve workers' rights and conditions.
- The Kaiser wanted to expand the German Empire, so he introduced Navy Laws (1898–1912) and used borrowed money to increase the army and navy.

⚙ APPLY

DESCRIBE

a   Define or briefly explain the following terms:

Kaiser	
Bundesrat	
Reichstag	
Militarism	
Socialism	
Navy Laws	

b   Make a list of problems or difficulties that Kaiser Wilhelm II faced in the years up to 1914.

c   Use your answer to Part a to write an answer to the following exam question:

> **EXAM QUESTION** Describe two problems faced by Kaiser Wilhelm II in achieving his ambitions for Germany before 1914.

EXAMINER TIP

Questions that ask you to 'describe' usually require you to write in detail about an event, situation or discovery. You should write down lots of factual information. For this question you should write about some of the difficulties that the Kaiser faced in paying for Germany's military expansion and the opposition he may have faced from other countries if he continued with his plans to expand Germany's empire.

REVISION SKILLS

Break down the information for the topic you are revising in different ways. You can create a brief fact file containing two or three important points about a person or key people.

Impact of the First World War

Germany and the First World War

The First World War began in August 1914. Germany and Austria went to war against France, Britain, Russia, Belgium and Serbia. More countries joined over the next four years.

Timeline: Germany's reactions during the war

▼ **In 1914**

■ The war was popular and patriotic Germans thought it would end quickly.

■ Soon the British navy stopped ships getting food into Germany, leading to food and other shortages.

▼ **In 1915–16**

■ In Germany, protesters demanded an end to the war. Demonstrations increased from 500 to 10,000 people. War weariness increased.

■ On the front line, soldiers were worn down by bombs, gas and machine gun fire.

▼ **Politically unstable**

■ Germany was close to defeat. A flu epidemic killed many already weak from a poor diet.

■ In October, Army General Ludendorff stated Germany could not win the war. He advised the Kaiser to make the country more democratic so the winning Allies (France, Britain and the USA) would treat Germany more fairly.

■ The Kaiser allowed the main political parties to form a new government, and transferred some of his powers to the Reichstag. But the German people were not satisfied and more demonstrations followed.

Defeat and the end of the monarchy

28 October 1918: The German navy in Kiel **mutinied**. The mutiny spread. Soldiers sent to deal with the protests also joined the sailors and workers. In just six days, workers' and soldiers' councils were governing towns and cities all over Germany. The Kaiser realised he had lost control. His army generals refused to support him.

9 November 1918: The Kaiser **abdicated** and secretly left Germany, never to return. Friedrich Ebert, the leader of Germany's largest political party (the SPD), took over Germany temporarily. He promised to hold elections and ended the war.

11 November 1918: Germany surrendered. The First World War was over.

Impact of the war on Germany by 1918

Virtually bankrupt

- Owed vast sums of money that it had borrowed to pay for the war.
- Lent some of its own money to its allies.
- Factories were exhausted.
- War pensions would cost the government a fortune.

Society divided further

- Some factory owners had made a fortune during the war, while workers had restrictions placed on their wages.
- Women worked in the factories during the war. Some people thought this damaged traditional family values.

Politically unstable

- There was mutiny and revolution all over Germany.
- Many ex-soldiers and civilians felt that politicians had betrayed Germany by ending the war.

Dolchstoss

The Weimar Republic

Temporary leader Ebert declared that Germany would be a **democratic republic** and arranged for elections for a new parliament to take place in January. A group of **Communists** in Germany, known as **Spartacists**, wanted Germany to be run by small councils of soldiers and workers. On 6 January 1919, the Spartacists seized power in Berlin.

↓

Ebert sent in a group of 2000 tough ex-soldiers, known as the Free Corps (Freikorps), to attack the Spartacists.

↓

After three days of brutal street fighting, the Free Corps recaptured buildings and arrested (and later killed) the Sparticist leaders.

↓

Ebert then held the elections and his own party, the SPD, won most votes and Ebert became the new German President.

↓

By now, the politicians were meeting away from the violence in Berlin in another German town called Weimar. They created the Weimar Constitution, which was a formal set of rules for how Germany would be governed. From this time, until the Nazi takeover, Germany was known as the **Weimar Republic**.

↓

In Weimar's new **Constitution**, which was a set of rules by which Germany was governed, all Germans had equal rights, including the right to vote.

What were the weaknesses of the Weimar Constitution?

 Proportional representation meant that lots of different political parties were able to win some seats in the Reichstag, but it was difficult for one party to get a majority. The leading party had to do deal with smaller groups in order to get anything done. This made law-making a very slow process.

 Many groups didn't like this new democratic system of governing at all. Some older army generals, judges, upper-class families, rich factory owners and university professors longed for the 'good old days' when the Kaiser ruled Germany.

 The new system of government and the politicians who created it were linked to Germany's defeat at the end of the First World War. Some Germans used the term 'November Criminals' to describe these politicians.

The constitution also contained **Article 48**, which meant that laws could be passed without the Reichstag by order of the President.

APPLY

IN WHAT WAYS

a Choose ten words that sum up the impact of the war on ordinary Germans.

b **EXAM QUESTION** In what ways did the lives of people in Germany change during the First World War?

EXAMINER TIP

Remember that this question is asking you to focus on the problems faced by ordinary Germans. Think about how their health, work and family life were affected by the war.

DESCRIBE

a How was the Weimar Republic formed?

b Who were the Spartacists?

c Complete the table below, outlining the strengths and weaknesses of the Weimar Constitution.

Strengths	Weaknesses

d **EXAM QUESTION** Describe two weaknesses of the Weimar Constitution of 1919.

EXAMINER TIP

If you are asked to describe two weaknesses, make sure you describe two.

The main political parties in early Weimar Germany

Names are in English but they have been given their German initials:

Political party:	Communist Party (KPD)	Social Democratic Party (SPD)	German Democratic Party (DDP)	Centre Party (Zentrum)	People's Party (DVP)	National People's Party (DNVP)	National Socialist German Workers' Party (NSDAP or Nazis)
Supporters:	Vast majority were working class	Mostly working class	Middle class, for example lawyers, writers	Catholics from all classes (southern Germany was mainly Catholic)	Middle class, mainly businessmen	Middle and upper classes, some ex-soldiers	Unemployed, many ex-soldiers; some support from middle and upper classes who feared communists

The Treaty of Versailles, 1919

The Treaty of Versailles was a list of punishments, instructions and orders that Germany had to follow because it lost the war. The Treaty stated:

> The war was Germany's fault, so Germany must pay for the war cost of the war (which was later set at £6.6 billion).

> Germany should only have a small army, a small navy, and no submarines, tanks or air force.

> Germany must hand over its colonies abroad to the winning countries.

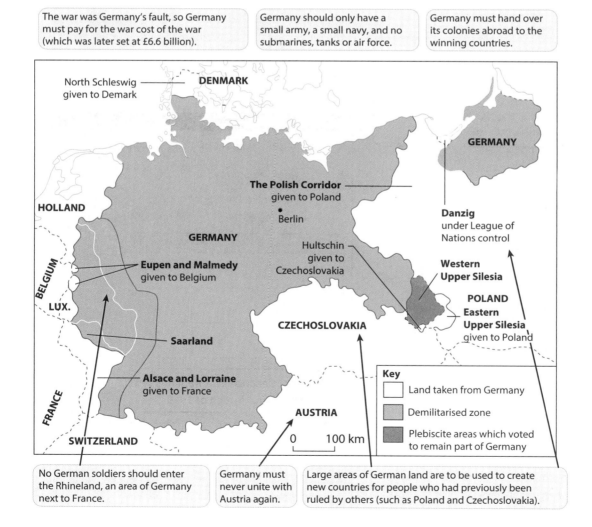

No German soldiers should enter the Rhineland, an area of Germany next to France.

Germany must never unite with Austria again.

Large areas of German land are to be used to create new countries for people who had previously been ruled by others (such as Poland and Czechoslovakia).

How did the Germans react to the Treaty of Versailles?

Germans hated the Treaty for three main reasons:

1 They felt it was too **harsh**. The Treaty took away large areas of land which meant losing people, factories, farms and mines. They had to pay a large amount of money to the winners too. Many Germans felt humiliated.

2 They were ordered to sign the Treaty, without discussion. They called it a '*diktat*' – a dictated peace.

3 Many Germans felt that they had not really lost the war at all! Instead, Germany's new politicians had **betrayed** the country by asking for a ceasefire when the Kaiser left Germany in November 1918. Some Germans, including soldiers, thought Germany could have carried on fighting, but was betrayed by the politicians who ended the war. Field Marshal Hindenburg said at the time, 'The German army was stabbed in the back. No blame is to be attached to the army. It is perfectly clear on whom the blame rests.'

 APPLY

INTERPRETATION ANALYSIS

a List four demands on Germany from the Treaty of Versailles.

b Explain why some Germans hated the Treaty of Versailles.

c Look at this interpretation of the Treaty of Versailles:

▼ **INTERPRETATION A** *Adolf Hitler, speaking about the Treaty of Versailles in a speech to the Reichstag, May 1933:*

> All of the problems causing today's unrest are a result of the Peace Treaty, which was unable to provide a fair, clear and reasonable solution for the most important questions of the time for all ages to come. None of this country's problems or the demands of the people were solved by this Treaty. As a result, it is understandable that the idea of a revision of the Treaty is essential. When I deal briefly here with the problems this Treaty should have solved, I am doing so because the failure in these areas inevitably led to the subsequent situations under which the political and economic relations between nations have been suffering since then.

- Summarise the author's opinion of the Treaty in one sentence.
- Can you suggest reasons why the author might have this view?

REVIEW

If you are unsure about how to analyse the interpretation, review the steps on page 8 on how to master your interpretation analysis exam skills.

EXAMINER TIP

An interpretation is a person's view about an event that has happened in the past. It might differ from another person's opinion about the event. It is your job to work out if it fits with what you know about the history of the event, and you will need to provide supporting evidence about why an interpretation might or might not be convincing.

EXAMINER TIP

You must remember that you won't get any marks for referring to the caption or the author (Hitler) in Question 3 about 'which interpretation is more convincing'. You only get marks in Question 2 for this, so avoid saying 'I disagree with this view or I find it unconvincing because it's written by Hitler.'

Reparations

In the Treaty of Versailles, Germany was ordered to pay **reparations** (payments for damages caused by the war) to the winning countries:
- In 1921, the figure was set at 132 billion gold marks (or £6.6 billion) to be paid in yearly instalments for the next 66 years.
- Later that year, the German government scraped together their first instalment of two billion gold marks and handed it over to France and Belgium. Some of the payment was in gold, but most of it was in goods like coal, iron and wood.

Occupation of the Ruhr, 1922

- In 1922, when the next payment was due, the Germans announced that they could not afford to pay.
- The French and Belgians didn't believe them and decided to take what they were owed by force.
- In January 1923, 60,000 French and Belgian soldiers marched into the **Ruhr**, a rich, industrial area of Germany. They took control of every factory, mine and railway in the region. They also took food and goods from shops and arrested any Germans who stood up to them.

Hyperinflation, 1923

- The German government ordered its workers in the Ruhr to go on strike and not help the French and Belgian soldiers remove goods from the country. This was known as passive resistance. The German government continued paying the workers on strike.
- The German government printed large amounts of money to pay striking workers and to pay the money they owed France and Belgium. This caused lots of problems. As workers spent money in the shops, shopkeepers began to put up their prices.
- The German government printed even more money to help workers buy products, so shops raised their prices again.
- Soon prices were inflating so fast that it became known as **hyperinflation**.

Year	Price of a loaf of bread	Price of one egg
1914		0.9 marks
1918	0.6 marks	
1923: Sept	1.5 million marks	4 million marks
1923: Nov	201 billion marks	320 billion marks

Impact of economic problems

By 1923, German money was worthless. Not surprisingly, many Germans blamed their government, because it was their decision to call a strike in the Ruhr and then to print so much money. For most Germans, 1923 was the worst year since the end of the First World War. Hyperinflation affected different people in different ways – but there were far more losers than winners:

Losers

 People with bank savings were the biggest losers. Some people had saved all their lives to get 1000 marks in the bank. By 1923, this wouldn't even buy them a loaf of bread.

 Elderly people who lived on fixed pensions found their income would no longer buy them what they needed.

 Many small businesses collapsed as normal trade became impossible because of the daily price changes.

Winners

 People who had borrowed money found it very easy to pay off their debts. They were the real winners. If a person had borrowed 10,000 marks in 1920 (a lot of money then), they could now pay off their debt with one banknote!

SUMMARY

What impact did the First World War (1914–18) have on Germany?

- It led immediately to mutiny in the navy and to the abdication of the Kaiser (9 November 1918).

- Germany became a democratic republic. The Weimar Constitution had both strengths and weaknesses.

- Weimar politicians ('November Criminals') were criticised by many for both surrendering in November 1918 and accepting the punishments in the Treaty of Versailles (June 1919).

- The reparations demanded as part of the Treaty crippled Germany. It could not afford to pay them.

- The demands of the reparation payments led directly to the hyperinflation crisis (1923).

APPLY

IN WHAT WAYS

a   Draw your own flow chart to show how the French and Belgian occupation of the Ruhr led to the hyperinflation crisis in Germany.

b   **EXAM QUESTION** In what ways were German people affected by hyperinflation?

EXAMINER TIP

Although hyperinflation had a very bad effect on most Germans, you must be careful not just to write about the negative impact of hyperinflation. Remember that some people gained from it.

REVISION SKILLS

Before beginning a question like this, you could make a short list of all the different ways in which hyperinflation affected ordinary Germans. Can you put these effects into categories, such as effects on income, savings, businesses, debts and so on? These rough notes could be used to create a plan to help you structure your answer properly.

CHAPTER 3

Weimar democracy

Political change and unrest, 1919–23

There were many murders, rebellions and uprisings against the Weimar government in the years immediately after the First World War.

The Kapp Putsch

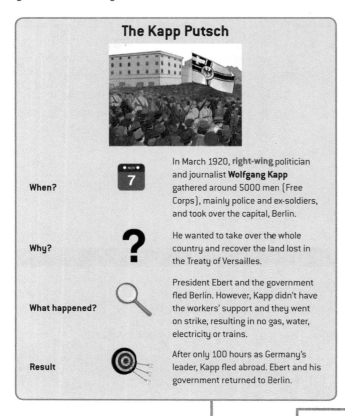

When? In March 1920, **right-wing** politician and journalist **Wolfgang Kapp** gathered around 5000 men (Free Corps), mainly police and ex-soldiers, and took over the capital, Berlin.

Why? He wanted to take over the whole country and recover the land lost in the Treaty of Versailles.

What happened? President Ebert and the government fled Berlin. However, Kapp didn't have the workers' support and they went on strike, resulting in no gas, water, electricity or trains.

Result After only 100 hours as Germany's leader, Kapp fled abroad. Ebert and his government returned to Berlin.

Assassinations

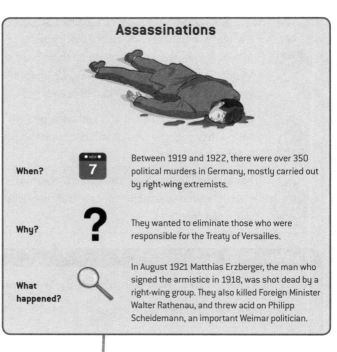

When? Between 1919 and 1922, there were over 350 political murders in Germany, mostly carried out by right-wing extremists.

Why? They wanted to eliminate those who were responsible for the Treaty of Versailles.

What happened? In August 1921 Matthias Erzberger, the man who signed the armistice in 1918, was shot dead by a right-wing group. They also killed Foreign Minister Walter Rathenau, and threw acid on Philipp Scheidemann, an important Weimar politician.

Murder, riots and rebellions, 1919–23

Red Rising in the Ruhr

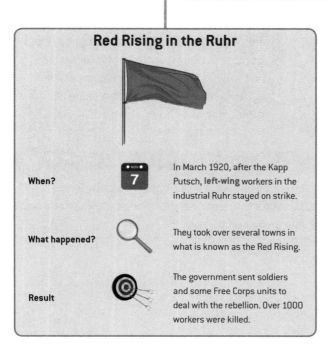

When? In March 1920, after the Kapp Putsch, **left-wing** workers in the industrial Ruhr stayed on strike.

What happened? They took over several towns in what is known as the Red Rising.

Result The government sent soldiers and some Free Corps units to deal with the rebellion. Over 1000 workers were killed.

The Munich Putsch

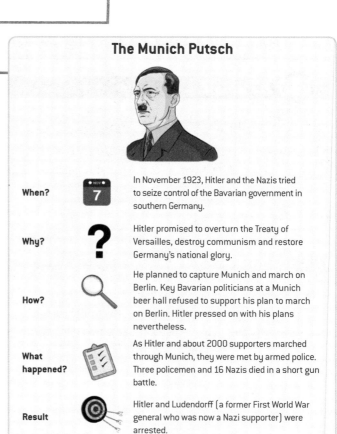

When? In November 1923, Hitler and the Nazis tried to seize control of the Bavarian government in southern Germany.

Why? Hitler promised to overturn the Treaty of Versailles, destroy communism and restore Germany's national glory.

How? He planned to capture Munich and march on Berlin. Key Bavarian politicians at a Munich beer hall refused to support his plan to march on Berlin. Hitler pressed on with his plans nevertheless.

What happened? As Hitler and about 2000 supporters marched through Munich, they were met by armed police. Three policemen and 16 Nazis died in a short gun battle.

Result Hitler and Ludendorff (a former First World War general who was now a Nazi supporter) were arrested.

- Germany had suffered during the war. Millions of ordinary Germans were poor and hungry.
- Many Germans believed they could have won the war. The Weimar politicians ('November Criminals') were criticised for agreeing to the armistice and accepting harsh punishments in the Treaty of Versailles.
- The Weimar government was seen as ineffective and unable to deal with Germany's problems.

 APPLY

BULLET POINTS

a Who was:
- Wolfgang Kapp?
- Matthias Erzberger?
- Walter Rathenau?
- Adolf Hitler?

b In the table below, briefly summarise each event and give each a rating of 1–10 to indicate how serious a threat it was for the Weimar Republic:

Threat	Date	Brief summary	Rating 1–10 (10 = greatest threat)
Kapp Putsch			
Red Rising			
Munich Putsch			

c

 EXAM QUESTION Which of the following was the more important threat to the Weimar Republic in the years 1919–23:
- left-wing risings
- right-wing plots?

Explain your answer with reference to both types of threat.

EXAMINER TIP

A good answer to this type of exam question will discuss each bullet point. In your conclusion you should explain which point had a bigger effect on Germany.

REVIEW

You should also include details on the Spartacist uprising. This information can be found on page 15.

INTERPRETATION ANALYSIS

Look at this interpretation of the Munich Putsch:

▼ **INTERPRETATION A** *Written by Rudolf Olden, a German lawyer and journalist, in 1936. During the Weimar period he was a vocal opponent of the Nazis and the writer of many books and articles banned by the Nazis after they came to power. He fled Germany in 1933 after Hitler's bodyguard unit, the SS, tried to arrest him:*

> Hitler wanted 'to make himself scarce'. This simply meant flight. At about noon a procession of 2000 National Socialists marched, twelve abreast, through the town. At first shot Hitler had flung himself to the ground. He sprained his arm, but this did not prevent him from running. He found his car and drove into the mountains.

a What impression does the interpretation give of Hitler during the Munich Putsch?

b Can you suggest reasons why the author might have written this about Hitler?

c Is it possible for historians to know exactly what Hitler did when the gun battle began? Give reasons for your answer.

EXAMINER TIP

For any interpretation, it is vital that you don't just work out what the person is saying, but why they might be saying it. Looking at the provenance (label) will help with this. Don't just look at who the author is; think carefully about the time they wrote or spoke, their intentions or intended audience, and the circumstances that allowed them to know about the topic or issue.

The Stresemann era (1924–29)

Between 1924 and 1929 Germany began to recover from some of its problems, and most historians put Germany's recovery down to the hard work of one man – Gustav Stresemann. Stresemann is best known as Germany's Foreign Minister from 1924 until his death in 1929. These are the main problems he faced – and how he dealt with them:

The hyperinflation crisis

He stopped the printing of bank notes and replaced the worthless notes with a temporary, new currency called the Rentenmark. In 1924 this was replaced by the Reichsmark, a stable currency that remained for the next 25 years. Hyperinflation ended. However, people who had lost their savings never got their money back, and blamed Stresemann.

French and Belgian troops in the Ruhr

He arranged for the USA to lend money to Germany (800 million gold marks). Germany then re-started its reparation payments. This 'deal' was known as the **Dawes Plan**. The French and Belgian troops left the Ruhr. However, some Germans felt Stresemann should have demanded a complete end to reparations. In 1929, through the **Young Plan**, Stresemann negotiated a reduction in the total payment.

Economic recovery

As well as using some of the borrowed American money to pay reparations, Stresemann also used it to build new factories, houses, schools and roads. This meant more jobs, with Germans earning more money. Slowly, Germany became more prosperous. However, some, even Stresemann himself, feared that Germany relied too much on the American loans.

Foreign policy

He worked hard to improve Germany's relationships with other nations.

- In 1925, Germany signed the **Locarno Pact** with Britain, France, Belgium and Italy. They promised never to invade each other.
- In 1926, Germany joined the **League of Nations,** an international peacekeeping organisation that Germany had been banned from when it was set up in 1919.
- In 1928, Germany signed the **Kellogg-Briand Pact**. The participating countries agreed never to go to war, unless in defence.
- Germany regained its international status and became an important part of the League of Nations. However, some Germans criticised Stresemann for not demanding back some of the land taken by the Treaty of Versailles.

Ongoing problems

Stresemann died in 1929. Germany had begun a new era of peace and prosperity under his leadership. However, there were still some underlying problems:

- There were many political parties. A government was made by several parties joining together. But they disagreed and wasted time arguing over decisions.
- Extreme political parties, e.g. the Nazis and the communists, did not support the Weimar system.
- Large groups of Germans were poor, e.g. farmers and middle classes who had lost their savings in the hyperinflation of 1923.
- German prosperity was built on American loans. What if they wanted their money back?

Weimar culture in the 1920s

The 1920s have been called a '**golden age**' for German artists, writers, poets and performers, who became known for their creativity and innovation. Before the First World War, the Kaiser kept tight control on all types of entertainment – but these controls were removed in Weimar Germany. Many people decided to experiment and try new things.

Cinema

Cinema became very popular. *Metropolis,* directed by Fritz Lang, was the most technically advanced film of the decade. German-born actress Marlene Dietrich became a global star playing glamorous, strong-willed women.

Nightlife

Germany became a centre for new plays, operas and shows. Musicians performed vulgar songs, about politicians, that would have been banned under the Kaiser. Berlin was famous for its nightclubs with live bands that played American jazz.

Literature

People had 120 newspapers and magazines to choose from. A German anti-war novel, *All Quiet on the Western Front* by Erich Remarque, became a bestseller.

Art and design

Avant-garde artists such as Otto Dix and George Grosz believed art should show the reality of everyday life, in particular the differences between social classes. In design and architecture, a new group of designers known as the **Bauhaus** believed in modern, practical designs.

Reactions to the changes

While some Germans embraced the changes, others hated them. They wanted culture to celebrate traditional German values. They thought the new nightclubs, shows and paintings were leading Germany into a moral decline.

REVIEW

The Nazis hated the nightclubs and art of this period. When Hitler came to power in 1933 he dealt harshly with them. Pages 50–52 cover this in detail.

SUMMARY

- There were many murders, rebellions and uprisings against the Weimar government immediately after the First World War. The reasons varied – from disgust with the Weimar government for agreeing to the armistice in 1918 to unhappiness with the government because it was seen as ineffective.

- In 1924 Weimar politician Stresemann began to successfully tackle some of the economic, social and political problems.

- The 1920s were a cultural 'golden age' with key developments in the arts, literature and design.

 APPLY

IN WHAT WAYS

a Who was Gustav Stresemann?

b Copy and complete this table:

Problem	Stresemann's policy	Success, failure or bit of both? Explain fully.
Hyperinflation		
French and Belgian occupation of the Ruhr		
Germany's poor relationships with other countries		
German industry short of money		

c EXAM QUESTION In what ways were the lives of Germans affected by the policies of Gustav Stresemann?

EXAMINER TIP

Try to reflect a range of impacts of Stresemann's economic and foreign policies.

DESCRIBE

a What is meant by the term 'culture'?

b EXAM QUESTION Describe what was new and exciting about Weimar culture in the 1920s.

CHAPTER 4

The impact of the Depression

What was the Depression?

From 1924 onwards, foreign banks, especially American ones, lent huge amounts of money to Germany to build factories and businesses. This created more jobs, more money and a better standard of living.

In October 1929 a financial crisis, known as the **Wall Street Crash**, hit the USA. American companies and banks went out of business, and millions lost their jobs. This soon became known as the **Depression**.

The impact on Germany

Economic

- Americans had bought many German goods such as cars, electrical equipment and clothing. But they couldn't afford these things any more because of the Depression, so German factories shut down. Millions lost their jobs.
- Troubled US banks demanded back the money they had lent to Germany after the First World War. German banks tried to reclaim this money from German businesses. They could not pay, and went bankrupt.

Social

- Many people were soon living on the streets – jobless, hungry and angry at their political leaders who they blamed for their problems.

Political

- People listened to different, often extreme, political parties (like left-wing communists and right-wing Nazis) that promised **radical** solutions to Germany's problems and ways of improving their lives.
- In the 1930 election, the communists increased their number of seats in the Reichstag to 77 (from 54). Nazi support increased from 12 seats in 1928 to 107 seats in 1930.

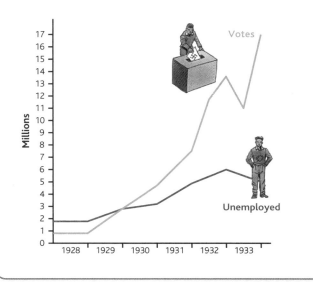

Reasons for the growth of the Nazi Party

In four years, the Nazi Party went from being the eighth most popular party in Germany to the most popular. In 1928 they won only 800,000 votes. In July 1932, they won nearly 14 million votes. The following diagram explores the factors (reasons) for this rise in popularity.

The Depression: By 1932, unemployment stood at six million. The Nazis promised to create jobs.

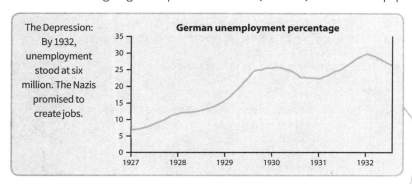

German unemployment percentage

Why did the Nazis become so popular?

Discontent with the Weimar government: Weimar politicians couldn't agree how to help the unemployed and get Germany out of the Depression. Several different Chancellors were appointed by President Hindenburg (first Müller, then Brüning) but they made little impact. Many ordinary Germans felt that the democratic system wasn't working.

Appeal of Hitler: With his charismatic personality, he convinced people that he could be trusted to make Germany a great nation. His powerful speeches filled his audiences with hope.

⚙ APPLY

DESCRIBE

a Write down 10 words or phrases that help describe the impact of the Depression on Germany.

b Make a list of reasons why you think people may have started to vote for the Nazis in the years of the Depression.

c (EXAM QUESTION) Describe two effects of the Depression on the German people.

INTERPRETATION ANALYSIS

▼ **INTERPRETATION A** *Adapted from an interview in the 1970s with Hans Kehrl, a German businessman who was a committed Nazi supporter and member of the SS, Hitler's bodyguard unit. At the end of the war he was sentenced to 15 years in prison for his role in the Nazi regime:*

> Well, really, it was the only party that promised to get us out of the hole and the idea was principally that it would only be possible if we developed as a nation a team spirit and solidarity, pulling all on the same rope instead of quarrelling about petty differences of opinion, foreign politics, social politics and so on. And they promised to do away with unemployment and build up agricultural life again and they thought that they could do this in the course of about five to six years, and as this was much better than anything else that was brought forward and as there was so much hopelessness I thought it was a real chance to follow them and their advice.

a In your own words, explain why Hans Kehrl decided to support the Nazis.

b In what ways is Hans Kehrl critical of the politicians of Weimar Germany?

Reasons for the growth of the Nazi Party (continued)

Why did the Nazis become so popular?

4 Fear of communism: German communists, such as the Spartacists, had tried to take over in the years after the First World War. This alarmed middle-class and wealthy Germans who didn't want to lose their wealth and position in society. Communists were anti-religion, which worried churchgoers. Hitler said he would fight communism and gained support from the middle and upper classes.

5 Nazi Party structure, methods and tactics:
After the failure of the Munich Putsch in 1923, Hitler changed tactics to legally win power in elections:

Nazi Party offices were set up all over Germany to recruit more followers.

The **SA (Stormtroopers)** protected Hitler's meetings and tried to influence voters at elections.

Hitler took part in mass parades and **rallies** to display Nazi power.

The Hitler Youth Organisation was set up to encourage younger followers.

The Nazis used new media like radio and cinema news reports, bought newspapers and printed millions of leaflets and posters to reach a wide audience. Joseph Goebbels, one of Hitler's most loyal followers, was put in charge of **propaganda** from 1928 to spread the Nazi message.

REVIEW ⟳

Refresh your memory about the Spartacists and the Munich Putsch by rereading pages 15 and 20 respectively.

Who voted for the Nazis?

Farmers

- The Depression hit farmers hard and the Weimar government offered little help.
- The Nazis promised them higher prices for crops, a better quality of life and higher status in society.
- Nazi opposition to communists appealed to farmers – if the communists took over they would seize farmers' land.

Women

- The Nazis targeted women voters by saying that family life, good morals and self-discipline were important.
- Some women agreed with Hitler's view that Weimar culture had been a bad influence on the young.

Middle classes

- The middle class – people such as small business owners, doctors, bank workers and managers – feared that law and order might break down during the Depression.
- They worried that a communist takeover could destroy their way of life.
- The Nazis promised to deal with problems decisively and the SA fought communists.

Wealthy classes

- The Nazis promised strong leadership to make Germany powerful again.
- Hitler promised to let owners run factories how they wanted, and his plans to build more weapons would be good for manufacturing.
- The communists wanted to take over many businesses, but the Nazis opposed them.

Youth

- Hitler's promise to tear up the Treaty of Versailles and make the country strong again appealed to young people.

- They wanted to be a part of Germany's bright future and get jobs in the armed forces or building new homes, motorways and hospitals.

SUMMARY

- The economic Depression, which began in America in 1929, affected many countries all over the world.

- Between 1928 and 1930, German unemployment rose from 2.5 to 4 million. By 1932 it was six million.

- Millions felt the Weimar government was doing little to deal with the crisis. Support for the more extreme political parties (like left-wing communists and right-wing Nazis) grew because they promised to solve Germany's problems.

- A number of other factors meant that support for the Nazi Party grew very quickly at this time.

- The Nazis appealed to a wide variety of people, including the unemployed, farmers, business owners and the middle classes.

APPLY

DESCRIBE

a Complete the table, writing two facts about each of the following reasons why the Nazis became popular.

Reasons why the Nazis became popular	Fact 1	Fact 2
The Depression		
Discontent with the Weimar government		
Fear of communism		
The appeal of Hitler		
Nazi Party structure and methods		

b Which do you think was the most important reason and why? Write your viewpoint, using no more than 50 words.

c **EXAM QUESTION** Describe two reasons why the Nazis became popular.

EXAMINER TIP

Be sure to connect each of your reasons to greater Nazi popularity.

BULLET POINTS

a Make a mind-map about the Nazis' popularity. Put 'How the Nazis became popular' in the centre, add branches with different reasons, and sub-branches to give more information. Use colour and drawings to make it even more visual.

b **EXAM QUESTION** Which of the following was the more important reason why the Nazis became more popular:
- the Depression
- the methods of the Nazi Party?
Explain your answer with reference to both reasons.

REVISION SKILLS

Mind-maps or spider diagrams are a good way of connecting different pieces of information. Draw lines between people or events and write on that line what links them.

The failure of Weimar democracy

RECAP

Political instability grew as the Depression worsened. As parties rarely won a majority in Weimar Germany, they usually got together to form a **coalition** government from which a Chancellor was chosen. Such coalitions were mostly ineffective and the President could use Article 48 of the Constitution to appoint a new Chancellor in emergencies.

Hitler's road to power

September 1930 Reichstag election

- No party won a majority so a coalition was formed.
- Nazis gained 107 seats to be the second largest party.
- Heinrich Brüning of the Centre Party became Chancellor. He was unpopular for cutting unemployment pay and raising taxes.

The September 1930 Reichstag election results	
Party	Seats won
Social Democratic Party (SPD)	143
Nazi Party	107
Communist Party (KPD)	77
Centre Party (Zentrum)	68

Hitler builds on success

1932 presidential election	
Paul von Hindenburg	X
Adolf Hitler	

- Nazis put up millions of posters and flags, and Hitler gave speeches at mass rallies – huge meetings – across Germany.
- Hitler's private army, the SA, beat up communists and disrupted their meetings, making it hard for them to campaign.
- Many Germans felt the chaos, violence and unstable governments proved that the Weimar government was failing.
- In March 1932 Hitler challenged Hindenburg for the presidency. He won an impressive 13.4 million votes against Hindenburg's 19.3 million.

July 1932 Reichstag election

- Brüning resigned in July 1932 and Hindenburg appointed another Centre Party politician, Franz von Papen.
- Von Papen lacked support, so he called an election.
- The results were astonishing: the Nazis were now the largest political party.

The July 1932 Reichstag election results	
Party	Seats won
Nazi Party	230
Social Democratic Party (SPD)	133
Centre Party (Zentrum)	97
Communist Party (KPD)	89

Another new Chancellor

- As a result of his success, Hitler demanded the Chancellor's job.
- Hindenburg refused because he thought the Nazis were a disruptive party and used his emergency powers to give the job to von Papen again.
- Von Papen called another election in November 1932. While votes for the Nazis fell slightly, they were still the largest party.
- Von Papen's Centre Party got fewer seats too, so he resigned again.

Hitler becomes Chancellor

- Hindenburg made his old friend Kurt von Schleicher Chancellor, but he had little support, so resigned.
- On 30 January 1933, Hindenburg had little choice but to appoint Hitler as Chancellor.
- He tried to limit Hitler's power by appointing von Papen as Vice Chancellor and only allowing Hitler to have two other Nazis in the cabinet.
- Hindenburg and his advisers thought they would be able to control Hitler.

SUMMARY

- The years after the start of the Depression were politically and economically unstable.
- Successive governments failed to deal with Germany's economic problems, leading to a series of elections after the resignations of ineffective Chancellors.
- Hindenburg used his emergency powers under Article 48 of the Constitution to appoint a number of different Chancellors.
- Support for the Nazi Party grew between 1930 and 1932. By 1932 it was the most popular political party but lacked the majority to make Hitler Chancellor.
- In January 1933 Hindenburg appointed Hitler as Chancellor but tried to limit his power.

 APPLY

DESCRIBE

a Write your own definitions for the following terms:

- majority
- coalition government
- Article 48.

b **EXAM QUESTION** Describe two ways in which President Hindenburg tried to resist or limit Nazi power.

EXAMINER TIP

In 'describe' questions, you do not have to explain *why* you have chosen the two ways – just describe them!

BULLET POINTS

a Copy out and complete the timeline below, making sure you include the various elections, Chancellors and key decisions between 1930 and 1933. Some sentence starters have been included to help you.

> September 1930   In the election...
>
> ↓
>
> January 1933   Hitler is finally...

b **EXAM QUESTION** Which of the following was the more important reason why Hitler was appointed Chancellor of Germany in 1933:
- the economic weakness of the Weimar Republic
- the political weakness of the Weimar Republic?
Explain your answer with reference to both bullet points.

EXAMINER TIP

The question clearly asks you to think about *both* the economic and political weaknesses of the Weimar Republic. A successful answer will not just focus on one.

REVIEW

Look back at pages 24–27 to refresh your memory about the Depression to help you answer this question.

REVISION SKILLS

Timelines are a simple way of covering the 'story' of an event in a visual way to help you remember key dates.

CHAPTER 6

The establishment of Hitler's dictatorship

Elimination of political opposition

As Chancellor, Hitler was not in complete control. President Hindenburg could easily have replaced him. Also, Germany was a democracy, so Hitler could only make laws with the Reichstag's approval – and over half of the Reichstag politicians didn't belong to the Nazi Party. However, Hitler quickly moved to increase his power and establish complete control of Germany.

 REVIEW

Retrace Hitler's route to the chancellorship in January 1933 by looking back at pages 28–29.

Timeline

▼ February 1933

- Hitler called a new election for March 1933, hoping to get a majority. He now had greater influence over many newspapers and radio stations. He used his control of the police to intimidate voters and beat up opponents.

▼ 27 February 1933

- A week before voting day, the Reichstag burned down. Hitler blamed it on a communist plot to take over Germany.

▼ 28 February 1933

- Hitler asked Hindenburg to pass an emergency 'Protection Law', giving Hitler the power to deal with Germany's problems. Because of the Reichstag fire and the apparent communist plot, Hindenburg agreed.

▼ March 1933

- The new law, the **Decree for the Protection of the People and the State**, banned leading communists from taking part in the election campaign. Four thousand communists were jailed and their newspapers banned. In the election on 5 March, the Nazis got more votes than ever, but still not the majority Hitler desperately wanted!

▼ 23 March 1933

- Centre Party politicians joined the Nazis. Hitler now had his majority. Many Centre Party politicians were bullied into passing the **Enabling Act** – he could make laws without approval from the rest of the Reichstag.

▼ 7 April 1933

■ Nazis were put in charge of all local government, councils and the police. The **Gestapo** (secret police) was formed. The first **concentration camp** for political prisoners was opened in Dachau, southern Germany.

▼ 2 May 1933

■ Hitler banned all trade unions.

▼ 14 July 1933

■ Hitler banned all political parties except the Nazis. The **Law Against the Formation of New Parties** banned the establishment of new ones. Germany was now a one-party state.

Voting Paper - July 1933
Put a cross next to who you want to run the country.

Nazis	☐
People's Party	☐
Centre Party	☐
Democrat P...	☐
Social Democrats	☐
Communists	☐

BANNED

▼ 2 August 1934

■ Hitler murdered his opponents in the SA during the **Night of the Long Knives** in June 1934. When Hindenburg died, Hitler immediately took over as President while remaining Chancellor. He made the army swear an **oath of loyalty** to him, and not to the country. Hitler decided to be called **Der Führer** – the leader.

REVIEW

Turn to the page 32 to read about the Night of the Long Knives.

⚙ APPLY

IN WHAT WAYS

a Make a set of revision cards that summarise how Hitler and the Nazis eliminated their opposition and achieved total power between January 1933 and August 1934.

b Give at least one example of how each of the following factors allowed Hitler to tighten his grip on power between January 1933 and August 1934:

- the use of law

- political scheming

- bullying and aggression

- chance and opportunism.

c In what ways were the lives of Hitler's opponents affected by his moves to become dictator of Germany?

REVISION SKILLS 📝

Revision cards are a good way of revising and creating a useful revision aid for later use. Jot down three or four things under a heading on each card. Try to include a factual detail with each point.

EXAMINER TIP ⟳

The question is not asking you simply to write about the moves Hitler made to become dictator – it is asking you to think about *how* those moves affected his opponents.

The threat of the SA

Despite now being in control of Germany, Hitler still felt he had rivals for power within the Nazi Party — and wanted to remove them. The most dangerous threat came from the SA, the very group that had helped Hitler achieve power.

The SA — from help to hindrance

- Had protected Hitler from harm and beaten up his opponents.
- Many SA members were violent thugs who wanted well-paid jobs as a reward now that Hitler was in power.
- Their leader was **Ernst Rohm**. Hitler worried that Rohm was becoming too powerful. The SA already had more members than the German army.
- Rohm wanted to combine the SA and the army, and control both himself.
- This alarmed Hitler and the army leaders. Hitler needed to keep the army leaders happy: he would need them to get back the land Germany lost in the Treaty of Versailles.

The Night of the Long Knives

Hitler dealt ruthlessly with the problem of Rohm and the SA in a series of bloody events on 30 June 1934. This became known as the Night of the Long Knives:

> Hitler arranged a meeting at a hotel in Bavaria, southern Germany, with SA leaders on 30 June 1934.

> Shortly before dawn, Hitler and an assassination squad from the **SS** (his bodyguards, the black-uniformed *Schutzstaffel*) stormed into the hotel and arrested Rohm and other SA leaders. They were later shot dead.

> Over the next few days around 400 political opponents were executed, including ex-Chancellor von Schleicher.

Impact of the Night of the Long Knives

- **Rivals dead:** Many of those who Hitler regarded as a threat were now dead, including Rohm and all the leading Nazis who didn't agree with Hitler.
- **Rise of SS:** The SS, led by Heinrich Himmler, was now responsible for Hitler's security, not the SA. Along with the Gestapo, the SS now formed the basis of the 'police state'. The SA remained but was never again a major force.
- **Rule of murder:** Hitler did not hide what he had done. His acts established murder as a method of the Nazi government.

- From January 1933, Hitler quickly increased his power and established complete control.
- Hitler used news media for propaganda and the SA to intimidate voters and beat up opponents.
- A number of laws limited personal freedom and allowed Hitler to govern without consulting the Reichstag.
- The Night of the Long Knives in June 1934 removed Nazi rivals, in particular SA leader Ernst Rohm.

 APPLY

DESCRIBE

a   Write no more than 20 words to define each of the following:
  - Ernst Rohm
  - the SA
  - the SS.

b   Create a 10-question test about the events of the Night of the Long Knives. You could even swap your test with a friend and test each other.

c

 EXAM QUESTION   Describe two consequences of the Night of the Long Knives.

Make sure you explain the impact of the two outcomes.

INTERPRETATION ANALYSIS

a   Create a spider diagram that outlines and assesses the Night of the Long Knives.

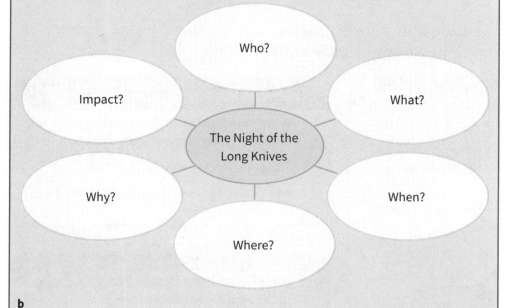

b

▼ **INTERPRETATION A** *From* Hitler Speaks *by Hermann Rauschning (1940); Rauschning was a disillusioned Nazi who left Germany in 1936 to live in America. Here he describes what he heard Rohm say in 1934:*

> [Rohm said] Adolf's a swine. His old friends aren't good enough for him. Adolf is turning into a gentleman. What he wants is to sit on the hilltop and pretend he is God. He knows exactly what I want. The generals are a lot of old fogies. I'm in the nucleus of the new army.

▼ **INTERPRETATION B** *Adapted from Professor William Dodd's diaries from 1941; Dodd was the American ambassador to Germany from 1933 to 1937. The response from von Neurath that he describes came in 1933, before the Night of the Long Knives:*

> The subject of SA atrocities came up. I spoke to von Neurath, the Foreign Minister, for an hour. [He] said 'the SA men are so uncontrollable that I am afraid we cannot stop them.' I requested a report from the Foreign Office about what the officials had done. No reply came, which I think means that the police have taken no measures against the guilty SA men.

 EXAM QUESTION

1 How does **Interpretation B** differ from **Interpretation A** about why the SA might be a threat to Hitler? Explain your answer using **Interpretations A** and **B**.

2 Why might the authors of **Interpretations A** and **B** have different interpretations about why the SA might be a threat to Hitler? Explain your answer using **Interpretations A** and **B** and your contextual knowledge.

3 Which interpretation do you find more convincing about why the SA might be a threat to Hitler? Explain your answer using **Interpretations A** and **B** and your contextual knowledge.

EXAMINER TIP ⊙

This interpretation question is worth the most marks, so give yourself enough time to answer it carefully.

CHAPTER 7

Economic changes in Nazi Germany

RECAP

Back to work

Over six million Germans were out of work when Hitler came to power in 1933. The Nazis set up a number of schemes, programmes and organisations to get Germans back to work.

The National Labour Service (RAD)

- All men aged between 18 and 25 had to spend six months in the RAD.

- They planted forests, mended hedges and dug drainage ditches on farms.

- They wore uniforms and lived in camps, but were given free meals and a small wage.

Public Work Schemes

- A new network of autobahns (motorways) to link Germany's major towns and cities was built.

- This gave work to nearly 100,000 people.

- New schools and hospitals were built, creating even more jobs.

'Invisible' unemployment

The Nazis used a variety of other methods to reduce unemployment figures:

- Women who gave up work to have a family did not count in the official figures.

- Part-time workers were counted as full-time.

- The Nazis created jobs by sacking people, such as Jews, and giving their jobs to non-Jews. These out-of-work Jews were not counted in jobless figures.

Rearmament

- The Nazis ordered the **rearmament** of Germany to rebuild its armed forces.

- New tanks, battleships, fighter planes and guns were built, creating thousands of jobs.

- Huge government arms contracts made factory owners and industrial bosses a fortune.

- Conscription was introduced in 1935. All males aged between 18 and 25 had to join the armed forces for at least two years. Within five years, the army grew from 100,000 to 1,400,000, creating even more jobs.

Nazi policies seemed to be working as unemployment fell steadily:

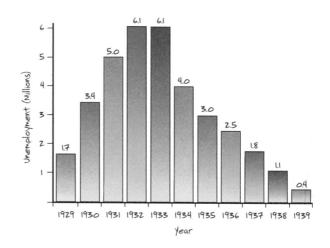

Work and control

The Nazis made great efforts both to control workers and to reward high production:

DAF: *DeutscheArbeitsfront* (German Labour Front)

- Replaced trade unions.
- Strikes now illegal, workers needed permission to leave jobs.
- Promised to protect workers' rights and improve conditions.
- Ran two schemes to improve Germans' lives: SDA and KDF

SDA – *Schonheit der Arbeit* (Beauty of Labour): tried to improve the workplace by installing better lighting, safety equipment, new washrooms, low-cost canteens and sports facilities.

KDF – *KraftdurchFreude* (Strength through Joy): organised leisure activities to encourage hard work. Had a reward scheme with cheap holidays, theatre trips and football match tickets if workers met targets.

The DAF also had a scheme to help workers save for a car. Hitler himself helped design an affordable 'People's Car', a Volkswagen. However, despite inspiring many people to work (and save) hard, the scheme was a swindle. No ordinary Germans ever received a car. Instead the money was used to build more weapons.

Better off or not?

The Nazis provided work – but workers lost their rights because trade unions were banned. Workers could not quit without government permission and strikes were banned.

People could also be forced to work as many hours as the Nazis required. One of the ways the Nazis created jobs was by sacking people, such as Jews.

The KDF did provide rewards for workers, such as holidays – but some holidays were still too expensive for most working-class Germans.

Food also cost more than it used to. Germany was trying to be self-sufficient and not rely on foreign imports. So with less food in the shops, shopkeepers charged more because of the high demand.

 **APPLY**

IN WHAT WAYS

a Make a revision card for each of the following terms. Jot down three or four things for each heading. Try to include lots of factual detail.
   - RAD: National Labour Service
   - DAF: German Labour Front
   - SDA: Beauty of Labour
   - KDF: Strength through Joy

b Create and complete a chart like the one below. The first line has been started for you:

Were ordinary German workers better off under the Nazis?	
Yes	**No**
The Nazis had promised plenty of jobs – and they delivered on this promise. For example…	Workers lost some of their rights because trade unions were banned. They could not…

c **EXAM QUESTION** In what ways did the lives of German workers change as a result of Nazi policies?

 EXAMINER TIP

The question does not just want you to list all the Nazi policies relating to work – you must also think about the effects that these changes had.

Economic policy

To achieve Hitler's goal of making Germany a powerful nation again, he wanted the Nazis to
control the economy and direct all manufacturing, agricultural and industrial production.
How would the Nazis achieve this?

The economy under Schacht

Respected banker Hjalmar Schacht was appointed Minister of Economics.

- He realised that imports of raw materials, such as iron, steel, rubber and wood, were needed to build more weapons.
- He signed deals with countries in South America and south-east Europe to supply raw materials in return for German goods.
- For a short time, things went well – weapons production increased and unemployment fell.
- But Germany was still dependent on foreign raw materials and the changes were too slow for the impatient Hitler.
- Schacht was sacked and replaced by Hermann Goering.

The economy under Goering

- In 1936 Goering introduced a **Four Year Plan** to increase military production.
- High targets were set (and met) in industries like steel and the production of explosives.
- However, targets were not met in other key industries like oil production.
- Germany still needed foreign raw materials so Goering tried to make Germany **self-sufficient**.

Self-sufficiency

The Nazis hoped to stop being reliant on foreign goods by making Germany self-sufficient.
They would find alternatives to the things the country needed, or develop artificial substitutes.

▼ German scientists found ways to make...

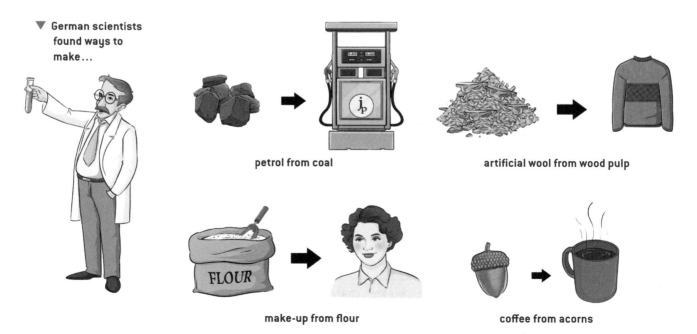

petrol from coal

artificial wool from wood pulp

make-up from flour

coffee from acorns

The Nazis and farmers

Around 30 percent of the population was involved in agriculture and forestry. Farmers had been important supporters of the Nazis. Although Hitler tried to reward their support by helping them cope with the Depression, his policies had mixed results.

Good for farmers

- Farmers' taxes were reduced.

- Farmers could not be thrown off their land if they got into debt.

- To keep farms large and controlled by the same families, farmers could not divide land between their children. This was popular with some farmers as it meant farms would be secure for generations.

Bad for farmers

- Some farmers did not like the law that prevented the division of farms because their children had to look for jobs in cities instead.

- In the late 1930s the Nazis controlled food prices.

 APPLY

IN WHAT WAYS

a Write a definition of the term 'self-sufficiency'.

b Make a spider diagram of the ways in which the Nazis tried to make Germany self-sufficient:

c **EXAM QUESTION** In what ways was Hitler's economic policy based on preparing Germany for war? Explain your answer.

EXAMINER TIP

Try to suggest the ways in which the targets and aims of the Four Year Plan would help Germany during wartime.

INTERPRETATION ANALYSIS

Look at this interpretation about Hermann Goering:

▼ **INTERPRETATION A** *From* Account Settled *by Hjalmar Schacht (1949). Schacht was Hitler's Minister of Economics and introduced the 'new plan'. He was dismissed from the government in 1943:*

> Goering set out with all the folly and incompetence of the amateur to carry out the programme of economic self-sufficiency. He exploited the powers Hitler had given him, as chief of the Four Year Plan, to extend his own influence. I had to denounce this economic nonsense, which I did in a speech to the Reich chamber of economics in honour of my sixtieth birthday.

a Who was Hjalmar Schacht?

b What is his opinion of Goering? Highlight all the words and phrases you can use as evidence to support your opinion.

c Can you suggest reasons why Schacht might think this about Goering?

REVISION SKILLS

Use sketches, doodles and pictures to help make facts memorable. You do not have to be a good artist to do this!

Impact of war

The Second World War (1939–45) went well for Germany to begin with. News from the war zones was always good as German forces won one great battle after another.

However, the war began to go badly for Germany. After defeat at the Battle of Stalingrad in Russia, German forces were pushed back on the Eastern Front. There were defeats elsewhere too, and then America joined on Britain and Russia's side. By the beginning of 1944, Germany was facing defeat and life at home had become very hard for ordinary Germans.

Hardship on the home front

Rationing

Supplies were needed for the soldiers, so there were severe food shortages:

Sold Out

- By November 1939, food and clothing were rationed. People were limited to one egg per week.
- Goods like soap and toilet paper were in very short supply.
- Hot water was rationed to two days per week.

Total War

In 1942, Albert Speer was made Armaments Minister. He organised the country for **Total War**: everything was focused on making weapons and growing food for soldiers. Anything that didn't contribute to the war was stopped:

- Beer halls (pubs), dance halls and sweet shops were closed.
- Letter boxes were boarded up.
- Factories stayed open longer.

Labour shortages

- Women were drafted in to work in factories as men were fighting the war.
- By 1944, around seven million foreign workers had been brought in to work as slave labour in the factories. They came from the countries Germany had conquered.

Bombing and refugees

From 1942, Britain and America began bombing German cities. As a result:

- There was no electricity, water or transport in many German cities.
- Thousands lost their homes.
- Thousands more left their homes to find safety as **refugees**.

SUMMARY

- The Nazis introduced a number of schemes, programmes and organisations to get Germans back to work.

- The German Labour Front (DAF) replaced trade unions. The SDA and the KDF attempted to improve the lives of German workers.

- The Nazis were determined to rearm Germany and make it self-sufficient. Great effort went into this, led by economist Hjalmar Schacht and later, Hermann Goering.

- The Nazis tried to reward farmers and save them from the worst effects of the Depression.

- The Second World War went well for Germany to begin with. The impact was felt strongly later in the war and ordinary Germans suffered with rationing, labour shortages and bombing.

APPLY

DESCRIBE

a Complete the table:

Hardship caused by war	Brief definition/ explanation	Impact on ordinary Germans
Rationing		
Total war		
Labour shortages		
Bombing		
Refugees		

b **EXAM QUESTION** Describe two ways in which the Second World War had an impact on ordinary German citizens.

EXAMINER TIP

Before starting a question like this, make a short list of the different things the Nazis did relating to the economy that might have helped Germany fight a war.

REVIEW

When thinking about the impact that the war had on German citizens, make sure you think about the information on pages 34–37 about how the build-up to the war had an impact, as well as the war itself.

INTERPRETATION ANALYSIS

a Look at this interpretation about the Ruhr valley:

▼ **INTERPRETATION A** *From* The Nazis: A Warning from History, *in which Johannes Zahn (1907–2000) was interviewed in the late 1990s. Zahn was a banker who was educated in Germany and then at Harvard University in America, he served in the German army from 1939–45. He was director of the World Bank from 1952–54:*

> One saw in the way the Nazis presented themselves as a welcome change to the earlier Weimar Republic. Rearmament helped to end the remaining unemployment so that the whole population was fully working, was earning and being fed. Rearmament also overcame the shame of surrender. We had a normal army again. You could thus say we were back to being an equal nation.

- What does Zahn suggest about Nazi economic policies?
- Why might he suggest this?
- How convincing is his interpretation?

CHAPTER 8

Social policy and practice in Nazi Germany

The Nazis and young people

The Nazis went to great lengths to control every aspect of young people's lives both in school and out. They believed that if young people were brought up to believe in Nazi ideas, they would become good Nazis who would never rebel against the regime.

Schools

- Teachers had to join the German Teachers League and teach what the Nazis wanted, or be sacked.
- Every subject was used to put forward Nazi propaganda and beliefs. So, in History, students learned how badly Germany was treated at the end of the First World War.
- Textbooks were rewritten to present Nazi beliefs as facts.
- Race Studies ('**Eugenics**'), was taught. Students were taught that the **Aryan** race was superior to others.
- PE became very important to prepare boys for the army. Girls studied domestic skills such as cooking and sewing to prepare them for their roles as wives and mothers.
- Students identified as potential future Nazi leaders were sent to special academies known as '**Napolas**' (National Political Educational Institutions).

Education under the Nazis

Universities

- Universities had to change their courses to reflect what the Nazis believed.
- Top university professors were hand-picked by the Nazis.
- Many lecturers were sacked, either for racial or political reasons. By 1939, over 3000 had been dismissed.
- All students had to train as soldiers for a month each year.
- The Nazis did not regard university education as particularly important, and fewer Germans attended university during the Nazi era.

Hitler Youth Organisation

As part of his campaign to **indoctrinate** the young with Nazi beliefs, Hitler set up the Hitler Youth Organisation (HYO).

Timeline

▼ 1922
Hitler Youth Organisation founded.

▼ 1933
All other youth groups banned. Of 7.5 million members, 2.3 million were aged 10–18.

▼ 1939
Membership made compulsory. Of 8.8 million members, 7.2 million were aged 10–18.

German boys

- Boys went to Hitler Youth meetings several times a week after school, and to special weekend camps every month.
- They learned how to march, fight with knives, fire a gun and keep fit.
- Activities were based on competition, struggle, heroism and leadership.
- The Nazis wanted to prepare the boys for their future role as soldiers.

German girls

- For girls the emphasis was on how to keep fit, cook good meals and care for babies, to prepare for motherhood.
- They also went on tough marches and attended weekend camps

REVIEW

Not all young Germans joined the HYO. Turn to page 54 to remind yourself about those who rebelled.

APPLY

DESCRIBE

a Write a brief explanation of the following terms:

- German Teachers League
- eugenics
- Hitler Youth Organisation
- Napolas.

b

> **EXAM QUESTION** Describe two ways in which the Nazis controlled the lives of young people outside school.

INTERPRETATION ANALYSIS

a Create a mind-map that explores how and why the Nazis changed the lives of Germany's young people.

b Look at this interpretation about education under the Nazis:

> ▼ **INTERPRETATION A** *Effie Engel, who went to school in Dresden, interviewed by the authors of* What We Knew: Terror, Mass Murder and Everyday Life in Nazi Germany *(2005); she was born in 1921 and came from a working-class family with close links to the German Communist Party (KPD) and the Social Democratic Party (SPD); in 1933 her father was a victim of the violent tactics of the SA:*

> The progressive teachers in our school all left and we got a number of new teachers. In my last two years of school, we got some teachers who had already been reprimanded. The fascists allowed them to be reinstated if they thought they were no longer compromised by anything else. But I also knew two teachers who never got a job again in the entire Hitler period. One of the new teachers was in the SA and came to school in his uniform. I couldn't stand him. In part, we couldn't stand him because he was so loud and crude.

- What is Effie Engel saying about the impact of Nazi policies on schools?
- Why might Effie Engel have this opinion?

REVIEW

Look at page 52–55 for information on propaganda and control.

EXAMINER TIP

Make sure you do not spend time explaining about schools in Nazi Germany – the question does not ask you to do this.

REVISION SKILLS

Reducing information to a more concise form is valuable. After reading a couple of pages of a textbook or your notes, ask yourself: 'What are the six most important things I need to remember?' Write those down on a piece of paper or small card. Don't worry about the things that you have left behind on the page – you'll remember those next time!

Women in Nazi Germany

The Nazis believed that the role women had to play in society was different, but equally as important, to the role of men.

Women in Weimar Germany

- In the 1920s, German women had many rights and freedoms that women in other countries did not have. For example, they could vote, and if they worked for the government, their pay was equal to men.
- Many women attended university and became lawyers and doctors.
- The birth rate fell as more women worked. In 1900 there had been over two million births per year. In 1933 there were under one million.

Women in Nazi Germany

- The Nazis were worried about the declining number of births. They felt that a low birth rate and a smaller population didn't fit with their plans to expand Germany's territory and settle Germans in other areas of Europe.
- The Nazis felt it was a woman's patriotic duty to stay at home, have lots of children and support their husbands.
- Women should stick to the three Ks – *Kinder, Kirche* and *Küche* (children, church and cooking)

Work

Many female doctors, teachers, lawyers and judges were sacked. Working was discouraged, as it might hinder producing children.

Family

Contraception and abortion were banned. Generous loans were given to newly married couples to encourage them to have children. The Motherhood Medal was awarded to women with the most children. Mothers with eight children received the 'Gold Cross'.

Nazi policies towards women

Behaviour

In many cities, women were banned from smoking because it was 'unladylike'. Wearing trousers or high heels was also frowned upon for the same reason. Slimming was discouraged because it might make it harder to get pregnant.

Sterilisation

The Nazis thought that some women were unfit to be mothers. The 'Law for the Prevention of Diseased Offspring' allowed forcible sterilisation of women with a history of mental illness, hereditary diseases or antisocial behaviour (like alcoholism).

Organisations

The German Women's League coordinated all adult women's groups, and representatives travelled around giving advice on cooking, childcare and diet. The Nazi Women's Organisation was an elite female group dedicated to Nazi beliefs and ideas.

Impact of the policies

- Thousands of women were prevented from following their chosen career path.
- The birth rate increased – around 970,000 babies were born in 1933, rising to 1,413,000 by 1939.
- When the Second World War started in 1939, there was a labour shortage as men were joining the army. Thousands of women were needed to work in factories for the war effort, taking on the joint role of main wage earner and mother. Unlike in Britain, though, women were still not called up to work.

 **APPLY**

DESCRIBE

a Write a brief explanation of the following terms:

- the three Ks
- Motherhood Medals
- German Women's League
- sterilisation policy.

b **EXAM QUESTION** Describe two Nazi policies relating to women in Germany.

BULLET POINTS

a Complete the chart.

Women before the Nazis	Nazi beliefs about the role of women	Nazi policies relating to women	Impact of Nazi policies

b **EXAM QUESTION** Which of the following were more affected by Nazi policies:
- young people
- women?

Explain your answer with reference to both groups.

 REVISION SKILLS

Mnemonics are useful memory devices to help you recall things such as lists of causes and consequences. Identify the keywords for the topic. Write them out. Rearrange them so that the initial letters spell something you can remember.

 EXAMINER TIP

'Bullet point' questions will often ask you to think about things you have studied separately. It is advisable to spend some time looking at the notes you have made on young people in Nazi Germany before attempting this question.

Nazi control of churches and religion

Most Germans were Christians. The Nazis and Christianity clashed because the beliefs and values of Christianity were very different from those of the Nazis. Traditional Christianity did not prosper under Nazi rule.

Germany's Christians

There were two main Christian groups in Germany:
- There were around 20 million Catholics (around one third of the population).
- There were around 40 million Protestants (around two thirds of the population).

The Nazis had to be careful with how they dealt with religion because it was an important feature of German society. But there were some key differences between Nazism and Christianity:

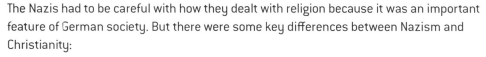

Nazism	Christianity
Nazis thought strength and violence were glorious	Most Christians believe in love and forgiveness
Hated the weak and vulnerable	Help the weak and vulnerable
Believed some races were better (superior) than others	Believe all people are equal in God's eyes
Hitler was a God-like figure	Believe in God and the teachings of Jesus Christ

Why did some Christians support the Nazis?

- The Nazis believed in the importance of marriage, the family and moral values. Most Christians believe in the importance of these too.
- Hitler had sworn to destroy communism. This appealed to Christians because communism was anti-religious.
- Hitler promised to respect the Church.

The Nazis and the Catholic Church

Hitler cooperated with Catholic leaders at first. A 1933 Concordat (agreement) with the Pope (head of the Catholic Church) said that the Catholic Church and the Nazis would not interfere with each other.

Hitler soon broke this agreement. Catholic priests were harassed and arrested and Catholic youth clubs and schools were closed down.

In 1937, the Pope issued his 'With Burning Anxiety' statement, read out in Catholic churches across Germany. This said that the Nazis were 'hostile to Christ and his Church'.

The Nazis continued to **persecute** Catholic priests.

In August 1941, Catholic Archbishop Galen (one of Germany's best-known religious leaders) openly criticised the Nazis. He was put under house arrest until the end of the war.

The Nazis and German Protestants

Hitler was admired by some Protestants, known as '**German Christians**', who wanted to see their Church under Nazi control.

Some Protestants were totally opposed to the Nazis. Pastor Martin Niemöller formed the **Confessional Church**, which openly criticised the Nazis.

Their leader, Ludwig Müller, became the first 'Reich Bishop' of the German Christians in September 1933. They often wore Nazi uniforms and used the slogan 'the swastika on our chests and the Cross in our hearts'.

The Nazis arrested around 800 pastors of the Confessional Church.

Niemöller was sent to a concentration camp and the Confessional Church was banned.

Other religious groups

- Jehovah's Witnesses were pacifists who refused to serve in the army. One third of Germany's Jehovah's Witnesses were killed in concentration camps.
- Members of other groups – the Salvation Army, Christian Scientists and the Seventh Day Adventist Church – were also persecuted.
- Jewish people suffered relentless persecution in Nazi Germany.

 APPLY

DESCRIBE

a Make your own version of the table of differences between Nazism and Christianity. Add a third column for any views they shared.

b **EXAM QUESTION** Describe two ways in which Christians reacted to Nazi religious policy.

BULLET POINTS

a Create a set of flashcards on the key facts about religious groups under the Nazis: Catholics, Protestants, Jews and other groups. On one side write the group and on the reverse write details about how they were affected by Nazi policies.

b **EXAM QUESTION** Which of the following were more affected by Nazi policies:
- women
- German Christians?
Explain your answer with reference to both groups.

REVIEW

Nazi persecution of Jewish people is covered in more detail on pages 46–47

EXAMINER TIP

Focus on facts when answering describe questions. These questions should not take you longer than a few minutes to answer in an exam.

REVISION SKILLS

Keep your revision realistic – you are unlikely to remember every piece of information! Think carefully about the type of questions you might be asked for each topic and ensure you can recall enough evidence when answering these sort of questions. Creating flashcards is a good way of doing this.

Racial policy, persecution and the Final Solution

Hitler believed that Germans were the 'superior' **master race** – Aryans – with the right to dominate 'inferior' races and groups of people. He feared that such groups would mix with Aryans and wanted to rid Germany of them. He had a particularly obsessive hatred of Jews.

Persecution of racial groups

- The Nazis classed Jews, Gypsies, Slavs (such as Russians), black and Indian people as 'inferior'.
- Hitler wanted to **cleanse** Germany of these people.
- The Nazis began to persecute and, later, murder members of these groups. Over half a million Gypsies and over six million Jews from across Europe died in death camps in the years up to 1945.

Persecution of 'undesirables'

- 'Undesirables' was Hitler's term for people with mental and physical disabilities and those who did not, in his view, contribute to society. He believed that they weakened Germany and he wanted to get rid of them to create a stronger nation.
- About 350,000 physically and mentally disabled people were forcibly sterilised by the Nazis. From 1939, the Nazis began to kill them. About 200,000 people, including 5000 children, were murdered in specially built 'nursing homes'.
- Around half a million homeless people, beggars and alcoholics were sent to concentration camps in 1933. Many were worked to death. Thousands of prostitutes, homosexuals and 'problem' families were sent to the camps too.

Shops
From January 1934, all Jewish shops were marked with a yellow Star of David or the word Juden (German for 'Jew'). Soldiers stood outside shops turning people away.

Early Nazi policies against Jews

School
Jewish children were forced out of German state schools and 'Eugenics' (Race Studies) was introduced in schools.

Laws
The Nuremberg Laws of 1935 banned marriages between Jews and non-Jews. German citizenship was also removed.

Work
From March 1933, all Jewish lawyers, judges, teachers (and later, doctors) were sacked.

Kristallnacht
In November 1938 Jewish homes, synagogues and businesses were attacked all over Germany and Austria. About 100 Jews were killed and 20,000 sent to concentration camps. Known as Kristallnacht (Night of Broken Glass).

The journey to the Final Solution

When war broke out in 1939, persecution of the Jews intensified:

- Jews were rounded up in some of the countries under Nazi occupation and forced to live in **ghettos** in major cities, or sent to work in labour camps.
- Execution squads (*Einsatzgruppen*) went out into the countryside and shot or gassed Jews.

The death camps

- At the Wannsee Conference in 1942, Nazi leaders planned what they called 'a final solution to the Jewish question': the mass murder of every Jew in Nazi-controlled territory.
- Heinrich Himmler, Head of the SS, oversaw the Final Solution.
- Six death camps (or extermination camps) were to be built. They contained gas chambers to carry out the murders, and large crematorioms to burn the bodies.
- Jews from all over German-occupied Europe were transported to these camps. In total, around six million were killed.
- The Nazis' attempt to wipe out the Jewish race is commonly known as the **Holocaust.**
- Thousands of Gypsies, homosexuals, political opponents, the disabled and any other groups whom the Nazis considered unfit to live were also killed in the camps.

Fighting back: Jewish resistance

- Some Jews fought back. They formed resistance groups, attacked German soldiers and blew up railway lines that the Germans were using.
- In some ghettos there was resistance — the Warsaw Ghetto Uprising of 1943 lasted 43 days.
- There were occasional rebellions in death camps. In Treblinka camp in 1943, 15 guards were killed and 150 prisoners escaped.

SUMMARY

- The Nazis tried to control all aspects of a young person's life. The school system and the Hitler Youth Organisation were dedicated to spreading Nazi propaganda and creating the sort of young people that the Nazis wanted.
- The Nazis believed that males and females had different roles: men as soldiers, women as homemakers.
- Some Christians supported the Nazis. But Nazism and Christianity often clashed because their beliefs were very different.
- Hitler believed that Germans were the master race and should dominate other races. He wanted to remove the groups he felt were 'inferior'.
- He especially hated the Jews and persecuted them harshly, with millions dying in death camps.

⚙ APPLY

INTERPRETATION ANALYSIS

a Write your own definitions of the following terms and phrases:

- master race
- 'undesirables'
- *Einsatzgruppen*
- Aryan
- ghetto
- Final Solution.

b Draw a timeline for the period from 1933 showing how the Nazis persecuted Jewish people.

REVISION SKILLS

A timeline is a good way to break down the information for a topic in different ways.

EXAMINER TIP

You will be able to use your understanding here to help you answer the interpretation question on page 49 about Germans and anti-Semitism.

CHAPTER 9

Control in Nazi Germany

It seemed that Hitler and the Nazis were supported by most Germans in the 1930s. However, the Nazis had such tight control over German lives that it is hard to tell how many people did not agree with their policies but were too afraid to say so. How did the Nazis create a climate of fear?

The police state

After 1933, Germany became a 'police state' – a country where the police and other organisations linked to the police (such as the courts) are very powerful and act on behalf of the government. The diagram on this page shows the different elements of the Nazi police state and how they worked together to control the country.

Himmler

- The Head of the SS.
- A loyal Nazi who personally reported to Hitler, whom he had known since 1923.

Heinrich Himmler

Regular police and law courts

- Ordinary police continued their work, but ignored crimes committed by Nazis.
- Top jobs in the ordinary police went to Nazis.
- Law courts and judges were under Nazi control. New laws meant that the death penalty could be given for, among other things, telling an anti-Hitler joke, having sex with a Jew, listening to a foreign radio station.

The Gestapo (secret police)

- No uniform.
- Spied on people they thought might be a threat. Tapped phone calls and opened mail.
- Had the power to arrest, imprison without trial and torture anyone.
- Set up a network of 'informers' who would report anyone who criticised the Nazis. Children were encouraged to report their parents or teachers.

The SS (*Schutzstaffel*)

- Set up in 1925, wore black uniforms.
- Originally Hitler's personal bodyguards, but over time divided into three sections:
  o The SD (*Sicherheitsdienst*)– looked after 'security'. They could arrest anyone for any reason, search homes and seize property.
  o The Waffen SS – elite unit in the army.
  o The Death's Head Units – ran the concentration camps, and later, the death camps.

Concentration camps

- Set up as soon as Hitler took power.
- Large prisons where any 'enemies of the state' could be held for any length of time. Anyone the Nazis didn't like was sent there – Jews, Gypsies, political opponents and anyone who criticised Hitler.
- Inmates were forced to work hard and some were even tortured or worked to death.

REVISION SKILLS

Try turning this diagram into flashcards as a way of revising the police state. On one side write the headings of each branch, and on the other briefly outline its role and the key facts.

⚙ APPLY

DESCRIBE

a What was a 'police state'?

b Write a sentence or two to explain:

- Gestapo

  _____

  _____

  _____

- Concentration camp

  _____

  _____

  _____

- SS.

  _____

  _____

  _____

c
> **EXAM QUESTION** Describe two ways in which the Nazi police state tried to control German citizens.

EXAMINER TIP

Remember that this question is not asking you to define the police state, it is asking you to think about the impact the police state had on the lives of ordinary people.

INTERPRETATION ANALYSIS

▼ **INTERPRETATION A** *From* The House that Hitler Built, *by Professor S.H. Roberts, published in the late 1930s. Roberts was an Australian Professor of History who travelled widely in Germany in the 1930s, met the Nazi leaders and attended Nazi rallies. His book publicised what was happening to the Jews and predicted another world war:*

> I saw young boys gathered around the anti-Semitic newspaper, *Der Sturmer*, gazing in admiration at the cartoons. I asked an SS officer whether he didn't think the newspaper was silly. He replied it is not. They must be taught the truth about the Jews. I looked at the cartoon showing a Jew disembowelling a beautiful German girl. I am impressed by the general agreement that such persecution of Jews is a good thing. I had expected many people to argue that it was unwelcome, forced upon them by propaganda or the pressure of events but this was not the case. I met nobody in Germany who apologised for the attitude.

a Summarise Roberts' views about German attitudes to Jews at this time.

b Why might he hold these views?

c How convincing do you find Roberts' views about German attitudes to the Jews?

 **RECAP**

Propaganda and censorship

Fear of arrest and imprisonment by the Gestapo or the SS helped the Nazis keep control. However, many Germans did not fear the Nazis at all and supported them fully. To make sure that as many people as possible continued to support them, the Nazis used two clever methods of control – propaganda and censorship.

Propaganda

- **What?** The spreading of information and ideas in the hope that it influences how people think and behave.
- **Who?** Leading Nazi Joseph Goebbels was put in charge of Nazi propaganda. He was a powerful speaker and very good at his job.
- **How?** He understood that propaganda worked best if people were repeatedly given some basic ideas with short messages and powerful images.

- **What?** Key messages:
  - blaming Jews for Germany's problems
  - criticising the Treaty of Versailles
  - making Germany great again.
- **How?** These messages continuously appeared all over Germany on posters, in newspapers, speeches, films and on the radio.

Examples of propaganda in Nazi Germany	
In newspapers	• Only stories that showed the Nazis doing good things were permitted. • There were negative stories about Germany's 'enemies'. • Newspapers that didn't comply were closed down.
In films	• All films had to show the Nazis in a good way, and their 'enemies' in a bad way. • Goebbels approved all storylines.
In books, at the theatre and in music	• Writers were forced to write books, plays and songs that praised Hitler and the Nazis.
On the radio	• All radio stations were under Nazi control to broadcast Nazi ideas. • Cheap radios were produced that could only tune in to Nazi-controlled stations. • Loudspeakers were placed in the streets, in factories and cafes to air broadcasts.
In public	• Impressive mass rallies were held to celebrate Hitler's greatness. • Huge arenas were built where carefully choreographed shows were put on with choirs, bands, speeches, fireworks and air displays. They were designed to impress and show how well organised the Nazis were. • Posters appeared all over Germany showing Hitler's power and the good things that the Nazis were doing.

Censorship

- **What?** The tight government control of what people hear, read, see or say.
- **Why?** Goebbels felt that propaganda wasn't enough to control what people thought. He wanted to stop ideas being shared that might challenge the Nazi message.
- **How?** The Nazis introduced strict censorship laws.
- **How?** Books, films, news articles, even jokes, were banned if they were viewed as harmful to the Nazis or Hitler.

 APPLY

DESCRIBE

a Make a series of revision flashcards that list the different methods used by the Nazis to spread their ideas. On one side write the method they used and on the reverse write details about how this method actually worked.

b Make a list of the ways in which the Nazis ensured that only *their* messages and ideas reached the German people.

c **EXAM QUESTION** Describe two methods that the Nazis used to control what information Germans received.

REVIEW

When considering this topic, look back at page 48 on the police state and pages 50–51 on culture under the Nazis to remind yourself of the full range of methods of control.

INTERPRETATION ANALYSIS

a Name three examples of messages that the Nazis spread through propaganda.

b Look at this interpretation about propaganda:

▼ **INTERPRETATION A** *From* The World at War *by Richard Holmes (2007), in which Lieutenant von Kleist-Schmenzin, a surviving member of the 1944 July Bomb Plot to kill Hitler, is interviewed:*

> I think a person who has never lived in a dictatorship can't understand the power of propaganda. If you just hear always the same, if you read in every newspaper the same and you have very few possibilities for other information then you become very impressed by the things which you are told. And it's very difficult to have to make up your own mind, to be critical.

What point does the writer of this interpretation make about the power of propaganda in Nazi Germany?

Art and culture in Nazi Germany

Cultural activities such as music, theatre, art and literature all had to reflect Nazi ideas and beliefs. The Chamber of Culture was set up to organise this.

Cinema

- Nazi supporters such as Alfred Hugenberg owned film studios, so the Nazis had a direct influence on exactly which films were made.
- Goebbels read and approved all film scripts.
- All films had to carry a pro-Nazi message.
- News reports of Nazi achievements were always shown before the main film.

Music

- Official approval was given to traditional marching music, folk songs and classical music by German and Austrian composers such as Bach, Beethoven, Mozart and Wagner.
- Some music that was popular in Weimar Germany was not permitted.
- Jewish composers were banned, and so was jazz music because it had its origins among African Americans.

Theatre

- In the Weimar era, Nazis founded the Militant League for German Culture to protest against 'modern' plays and films they disapproved of.
- When the Nazis took over, they ruled that plays should mainly focus on German history and politics.
- Songs about sex and politics were common in Germany's cabaret clubs. The Nazis closed them down.

The Chamber of Culture

- Led by Joseph Goebbels.
- All musicians, writers, artists and actors had to be members.
- Anyone who refused would not be allowed to work.
- Some people, such as Jews, were banned from joining.

Literature

- A list of banned books was created. 'Un-German' books or those by Jewish authors were removed from libraries and bookshops. Goebbels organised events in which books were gathered and burned.
- Goebbels encouraged books about race, the glory of war and the brilliance of the Nazis.
- Some popular books written in Weimar Germany were banned, including Erich Remarque's anti-war novel *All Quiet on the Western Front*
- Hitler's *Mein Kampf* was the bestselling book in Germany.
- Around 2500 writers left Germany between 1933 and 1945.

Art

- The Nazis wanted art to be clearly understandable to ordinary people. It should show healthy, heroic German figures and family scenes of happy, strong, 'pure' Germans.
- Hitler hated modern art and called it 'degenerate' (perverted).
- In 1936, the Nazis publicly burned 5000 paintings they disapproved of. They put on an exhibition of 'degenerate' art to mock it and opened another of officially approved paintings.

Design

- Hitler had clear ideas about the design of big, public buildings like libraries, government offices and parade grounds. He favoured huge, stone structures, often copies of buildings from ancient Greece or Rome.
- 'Bauhaus' was an important architectural and design movement in Weimar Germany. It used new technology to design simple, practical buildings and objects. Hitler did not approve of such modern design, and closed the movement down in 1933.

Sports and leisure

- Health and physical fitness was important to the Nazis, so success in sport was used to promote the Nazi regime.
- The Olympic Games, held in Berlin in 1936, was a propaganda opportunity. Famous German filmmaker Leni Riefenstahl made a groundbreaking film of the Games using the latest German technology.
- The German team came top of the medals table. The Nazis claimed that this showed the superiority of the German race.
- During the Games, anti-Semitic posters and newspapers were temporarily stopped to give the rest of the world the impression of a more tolerant Germany.

 APPLY

DESCRIBE

a Write a sentence to explain each of the following:

- the Chamber of Culture
- the Militant League for German Culture
- the 'Bauhaus' movement.

b **EXAM QUESTION** Describe two ways in which the Nazis controlled German arts and culture.

 REVIEW

To refresh your memory about the Weimar culture that the Nazis disliked so much, look back at pages 22–23.

BULLET POINTS

a Copy and complete this table:

Cultural activity	How was this changed by the Nazis?	Why do you think they changed it?
Cinema		
Music		
Theatre		
Literature		
Art		
Design		
Sport		

b **EXAM QUESTION** Which of the following was the more important reason why the Nazis were able to control the people of Germany:

- the police state
- propaganda?

Explain your answer with reference to both reasons.

 EXAMINER TIP

'Bullet point' questions will often ask you to think about things you have studied separately. It is advisable to spend some time looking at the notes you have made on young people in Nazi Germany before attempting this question.

INTERPRETATION ANALYSIS

▼ **INTERPRETATION A** *From* The Goebbels Diaries, *edited by Louis Lochner (1948). Lochner, an American journalist, witnessed the first burning of books in 1933. He reported for American papers with the German army on the Western Front but was imprisoned in 1941 when America joined the war:*

> On 10 May the whole civilised world was shocked when the books of authors displeasing to the Nazis were burned here in Berlin. All afternoon Nazi raiding parties are gone into the public and private libraries throwing onto the street any books which Dr Goebbels, in his supreme wisdom, had decided were unfit for Nazi Germany.

a Summarise Lochner's view about Nazi censorship.
b Why might he hold those views?

 EXAMINER TIP

Think about how Lochner's background as an American and journalist might influence his views.

Resistance and opposition

The Nazis had a firm grip on Germany with its methods of propaganda, censorship and intimidation, but opposition remained. There were different levels of challenge to the Nazis in Germany:

Type of resistance	Examples
'Grumbling' or moaning 	The lowest type of opposition. • In the privacy of their own homes, people might tell an anti-Nazi joke or complain about the Nazi regime.
Passive resistance 	A public show of opposition, often by refusing to do what most of the population were doing. • Some might refuse to give the 'Heil Hitler' salute or to give money to the Hitler Youth members who were collecting funds.
Open opposition 	Some Germans organised themselves into groups to openly oppose the Nazis. • The **Swing Youth** declared their dislike of Nazi ideas and policies by listening to jazz music and having Jewish friends. • The **White Rose group,** led by brother and sister Hans and Sophie Scholl, urged Germans to get rid of Hitler. They handed out anti-Nazi leaflets, put up posters and wrote graffiti on walls. • Youth groups such as the **Edelweiss Pirates** and the Navajos beat up Nazi officials and helped army deserters. • Other groups sabotaged railway lines and passed on military secrets to other countries. Protestant and Catholic Church leaders made some open criticism of the Nazis too. • The Catholic Church spoke out in 1941 against the killing of physically and mentally disabled people.
Attempts to kill Hitler 	There were around 50 attempts on Hitler's life, some by lone individuals, and others by organised groups: • The Kreisau Circle – a group of army officers, university professors and aristocrats who discussed assassinating Hitler, but didn't actually do anything. • The Beck-Goerdeler group – contacted the British about removing Hitler, but no agreement was reached. The group did, however, try to kill Hitler in March and November 1943, and was behind the July Bomb Plot of 1944. • The July 1944 Bomb Plot – army officer Colonel Claus von Stauffenberg was part of a group that detonated a bomb where Hitler was meeting other Nazi leaders. Despite killing four men and injuring Hitler, the bomb failed to kill him.

REVIEW

Look back at pages 44–45 to remind yourself about Church opposition to the Nazis.

SUMMARY

- Under the Nazis, Germany became a police state.

- The Nazis used the police force and the justice system in an attempt to terrorise ordinary Germans into conforming.

- Some Germans supported the Nazi regime because they believed in their aims.

- The Nazis also used propaganda and censorship to help them control people and spread the Nazi message.

- Cultural activities – music, theatre and literature, for example – had to reflect Nazi ideas and beliefs. Any cultural activities that did not support the Nazis were banned, including many from the Weimar period.

- Despite the use of propaganda, censorship and intimidation, opposition to the Nazis remained. There were different levels of opposition, ranging from passive resistance to open opposition and attempts to kill Hitler.

 APPLY

DESCRIBE

a Create a mind-map, with four branches – 'Grumbling' or moaning, Passive resistance, Open opposition, and Attempts to kill Hitler. From each branch, write a definition of each type of resistance and explain why people resisted in this way.

b Can you suggest reasons why so little was achieved by the resistance to Hitler?

c Describe two ways in which the German people resisted and opposed Hitler and the Nazis.

REVISION SKILLS

Record yourself on your phone (or other device) reading your notes. Play back the information when you are travelling or waiting for something.

INTERPRETATION ANALYSIS

▼ **INTERPRETATION A** *Adapted from William Shirer's book,* The Rise and Fall of the Third Reich, *1960. Shirer was an American journalist who reported from Berlin, Germany between 1934 and 1940:*

The German people had to put up with radio programmes and films that were just as stupid and boring as their daily newspapers. They stayed away from Nazi films and went to cinemas showing those few foreign films, mostly from Hollywood, that Goebbels allowed. In the mid-1930s hissing at German-made films was so common that Frick, Minister for the Interior, warned against 'treasonable behaviour by cinema audiences'. Radio programmes were criticised so much that the president of the Radio Chamber said that such comments were 'an insult to German culture' and would not be tolerated.

a What is the author's view of German newspapers, radio and film?

b Why might the author have this view?

c How convincing do you find the author's view about Nazi art and media?

REVIEW

You may wish to look back at pages 48–52 to remind yourself about propaganda, arts and the Nazi police state.

EXAMINER TIP

Consider the author's background, job and expectations.

GCSE sample answers

 **REVIEW**

On these exam practice pages, you will find a sample student answer for each of the question types you will find in the Germany section of your Paper 1 exam. What are the strengths and weaknesses of the answers? Read the following pages and think carefully about what the student has written, what the examiner has said about each answer, and how you might improve your own answers to the Germany exam questions.

Interpretation analysis questions

Paper 1, Section A begins with three questions that ask you to work with two interpretations and their accompanying provenance (caption or label).

The interpretations in Paper 1 are by people who have lived through the events they are referring to. They are speaking *at least* five years after the events have taken place.

You will be asked three interpretations questions:

- The first question asks *how* the interpretations differ.
- The second question asks you to explain *why* they might differ.
- The third question asks you to *evaluate* what each interpretation has to say about the history involved.

▼ **INTERPRETATION A** *Henrik Metelmann, speaking in a BBC documentary series in 1997 about his experiences in the Hitler Youth in the 1930s. Henrik joined the Hitler Youth as an 11-year-old. He was from a poor working-class area of Hamburg. He went on to join the German army and fought all through the war:*

> I simply loved it in the Hitler Youth. The uniform was so smashing – the dark brown, the black, the swastika. I loved marching, the flag before us, the drum beating the pace. Most roads in Germany at that time had cobbles, and it was painful on our feet, but that didn't matter, we felt important. The police had to stop traffic to give us right of way and passers-by had to salute to respect our flag. I remember how funny it was to see old ladies with their shopping bags shooting their arms up into the air.

▼ **INTERPRETATION B** *Adapted from an account written in the 1950s by a young German, Arno Klönne, whose parents were teachers and had access to banned books. In his account he remembers his time in the Hitler Youth during 1940. After the war, Klönne went on to be become a university professor and had an important job with a socialist newspaper in Germany:*

> When I was older, I became a Hitler Youth leader. I found the need for absolute obedience unpleasant. The Nazis preferred people not to have a mind of their own. In our troop the activities consisted almost entirely of endless military drill. Even if sport or shooting practice or a singsong was planned, we always had to drill first.

EXAMINER TIP

While reading the interpretations, try to think about the key point each one makes and then how they are different from each other. Why not make notes around them or underline the things that are different? This is excellent preparation for the first of the three questions.

EXAMINER TIP

It is really important to think about some possible reasons *why* the two interpretations might differ. Remember that an interpretation is a person's view about something at least five years after they have lived through it. There will be reasons why they hold that particular view – and this is what you need to identify for the second of the three questions. You should read the provenance for each of the interpretations carefully because it will contain clues as to why the person thinks a certain way.

1 How does **Interpretation B** differ from **Interpretation A** about life for young people in Nazi Germany? Explain your answer using **Interpretations A** and **B**.

4 marks

EXAMINER TIP

This question is very straightforward and is worth 4 marks. The examiner will be looking to see if you understand the differences between the two interpretations.

Now look at a student answer. Remember, this question is asking you to write about the ways in which the two interpretations are different.

Sample student answer

Interpretation A focuses on the positive side of being in the Hitler Youth. Henrik Metelmann said how much he loved it in the Hitler Youth and gives reasons why he enjoyed it so much. He talks about the pleasure he felt at the approval and attention he received and how much he liked marching along the roads. He liked it even though the cobbled roads hurt his feet.

Interpretation B is different because this person says they didn't like it so much in the Hitler Youth.

EXAMINER TIP

The student broadly identifies the differences — that the writer of Interpretation A loved it in the Hitler Youth while the author of Interpretation B didn't.

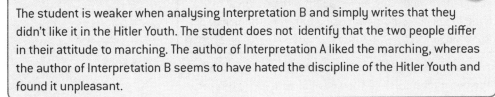
EXAMINER TIP

The student is weaker when analysing Interpretation B and simply writes that they didn't like it in the Hitler Youth. The student does not identify that the two people differ in their attitude to marching. The author of Interpretation A liked the marching, whereas the author of Interpretation B seems to have hated the discipline of the Hitler Youth and found it unpleasant.

OVERALL COMMENT

This would achieve a Level 2 mark for the extended reasoning applied to Interpretation A.

 2 Why might the authors of **Interpretations A** and **B** have a different interpretation about life for young people in Nazi Germany? Explain your answer using **Interpretations A** and **B** and your contextual knowledge.

4 marks

EXAMINER TIP

It is vital that you look at who the author is, the time when they were writing or speaking, their intentions and intended audience. You will never really know why they said what they said, so you have to speculate. However, your answer can still be historically informed. There is no need to repeat WHAT is different in the two interpretations (you have already done that in question 1) — instead just focus on why!

Look at the student answer. Remember, this question is asking you to write about WHY the interpretations are different. As a result, you will have to read the provenance very carefully.

Sample student answer

The author of Interpretation A is clearly keen on Hitler and the Hitler Youth. As a young boy he would have been brainwashed at school and in his Hitler Youth meetings so is probably very keen on the idea of serving Hitler and the Nazi Party. He seems very proud to wear the uniform. Also, as a young boy from a poor background, he may have been attracted to the activities and status of the Hitler Youth because he may never have done anything like this before.

The author of Interpretation B finds the discipline of the Hitler Youth unpleasant. This might be to do with his background. His parents were teachers who could get books that were banned so at home he was able to think for himself and have a mind of his own. He was in the Hitler Youth after the Second World War had started when the experience was much more military as his account indicates. He was not as brainwashed as the author of Interpretation A because he had parents who had risked arrest for keeping banned books so they probably talked to him about politics other than Nazi politics.

EXAMINER TIP

The student uses conditional words such as 'probably', 'may have', 'might be' and 'seems'. Such a speculative approach is good when not all the facts are known.

OVERALL COMMENT

This is a good Level 1 answer. There are other aspects of the provenance, such as the dates and occupation of the authors, that could be explored for Level 2. The answer explains reasons why each author might think as they do. Given the background of A, he was poor and enjoyed the status. For B the answer identifies the time – wartime – when the experience in the Hitler Youth was different to that of A. Also he may have been less likely to be brainwashed as B was more educated and had a better home life.

EXAM QUESTION

3 Which interpretation do you find more convincing about Hitler's appeal to the young people of Germany? Explain your answer using **Interpretations A** and **B** and your contextual knowledge. **8 marks**

This question uses the key word 'convincing'. So, your answer should not focus on the differences or the provenance of the two interpretations (you have already done this). Instead, this time you need to focus on the history surrounding the issue mentioned in the question – in this case, 'Hitler's appeal to the people of Germany'.

In simple terms, you are being asked which interpretation is better – which one 'fits in' with what you have learned. One way to look at it is to think of the two interpretations as witnesses in a trial – which version, based on all you have learned in the topic, is most believable (or 'convincing'). Now look at the student answer.

Sample student answer

Firstly, Interpretation A is quite convincing because young people were targeted in Hitler's Germany and brainwashed into thinking that Hitler and the Nazis were the best thing that had ever happened to Germany. Hitler used organisations like the Hitler Youth to make sure that young people were loyal to him from a very early age so that they would be prepared to put up with hardships that may come – and even be prepared to die for him. For example, in schools all teachers who did not support the Nazis were sacked. All subjects in schools had the same aim – to prepare boys to be tough, hard soldiers of the future and prepare girls to be wives and mothers. This was carried on after school in the Hitler Youth movement, where young boys and girls were trained in military skills and girls were trained to look after the men and value having a large family. The author of Interpretation A seems to have been brainwashed like so many young people in Hitler's Germany.

Interpretation B is quite convincing too because I know that not every young person was happy with Hitler and the Nazis. There were many people who opposed him, either by joining a banned youth group like the Edelweiss Pirates or by doing small acts of resistance like keeping banned books (like this person's parents) or failing to give the 'Heil Hitler' salute.

I think, though, that Interpretation A is more convincing because I think that most young people were like Henrik. There were some like Arno, but not many.

OVERALL COMMENT

This answer reaches Level 3 because it has detailed and specific knowledge about both interpretations.

OVER TO YOU

Read the sample answers again, but this time:

a   In Answer 1, highlight where it specifically mentions the *differences* between the two interpretations.

b   In Answer 2, highlight where it gives reasons *why* the two interpretations are different.

c   In Answer 3, highlight where it demonstrates factual knowledge.

d   Finally, have a go at writing a series of answers yourself, making sure you closely follow the advice given here. You should spend about 5 minutes on question 1, 5 minutes on question 2 and 10 minutes on question 3.

The 'describe' question

 4   Describe two problems Hitler faced as Germany's leader when he became Chancellor in January 1933.   **4 marks**

Sample student answer

One of Hitler's problems was that he was not very secure as Chancellor. He owed his job to President Hindenburg, who could use his emergency powers if he wanted to sack him and replace him with another Chancellor. Hindenburg had already changed Chancellors several times already and Hitler could be replaced in the same way. Hindenburg had even appointed von Papen as Vice Chancellor and restricted the number of Nazis in the cabinet to two in an attempt to limit Hitler's power.

Another problem for Hitler was Germany's democratic system. Hitler could only make laws if the majority of Reichstag politicians agreed to them. However, more than half the Reichstag politicians did not belong to the Nazi Party so Hitler would struggle to pass laws and make changes without the support of a majority. This was a problem because Hitler's power was limited, which was a problem for a politician who had promised so much change.

OVERALL COMMENT

This is a top-level answer – it would achieve Level 2. The **key to reaching the higher marks** is not **just** to write down lots of factual information about the problem, the issue or the feature, but you must also ensure that the answer explains why the aspect identified was a problem– the student has shown this in this answer.

OVER TO YOU

1   How would you improve the sample answer?

2   Now it's time for you to have a go at planning and writing an answer to this question. Spend no more than five minutes on your answer.

3   Now check your answer…

☐   Did you name two problems?

☐   For each problem, did you **expand** on it and **explore why** it was a problem for Hitler?

If you are struggling to remember events in Germany before the First World War, reread pages 12–13 of this Revision Guide.

The 'in what ways' question

 5   In what ways were the lives of young people affected by Nazi policies? Explain your answer.

[8 marks]

EXAMINER TIP

The 'in what ways' question is not an essay question – the aim is that you quickly write down the ways in which the Nazis *changed* the lives of young people.

Sample student answer

The lives of young people were affected a lot by Nazi policies. The Nazis tried to control all parts of a young person's life in school and outside of it. They thought that if young people were brought up to believe in Nazi ideas, then they would grow up to be good Nazis who would never rebel against the regime.

To start, the Nazis used schools to brainwash youngsters into loving Hitler and the Nazi Party. For example, in History, students would learn how badly Germany was treated at the end of the First World War and in Maths lessons students would calculate how much money Germany would save if it got rid of all disabled people. There was lots more PE in schools than there ever

EXAMINER TIP

The student has chosen to focus on two areas: the way Nazis changed schools and the way they changed lives after the school day was over. But the answer needs to be more specific about the ways in which this was done.

EXAMINER TIP

If you say that the growth of trade unions was a problem for the Kaiser, don't just leave it there. Make sure you go into detail about why the growth of trade union membership was a problem for the Kaiser. In other words, what were the potential consequences of increased membership for the Kaiser? Other 'problems' you might identify could be the problems associated with the debt that Germany was finding itself in as a result of the Navy Laws and the policy of Weltpolitik, or you might write about the growth of socialism (and the SPD) and the potential threat this had on the Kaiser's power.

EXAMINER TIP

It is good that the student has remembered how individual subjects were changed. However, this is supporting information for a point that has not been made! The student should have linked the 'brainwashing' with the point about *how* they did this. For example, 'the Nazis changed the school curriculum, adding subjects and the time spent on them, to make sure that they put forward Nazi ideas'.

had been to prepare boys for life in the army. Girls were taught about cooking and home-making to prepare them for lives as wives and mothers.

Eugenics (or Race Studies) was taught too. This new subject taught how to improve the race and focused on the Nazi belief that some races were superior to others. This meant that young people grew up believing that they were better than other races.

The Nazis wanted control of young people outside school too. The Hitler Youth Organisation was set up to teach boys military skills with an emphasis on competition, struggle and leadership. The Nazis wanted to prepare the boys for their future role as soldiers. Girls also went on tough marches and attended weekend camps, but they would mainly learn how to keep fit, cook good meals and look after babies, to prepare for motherhood.

EXAMINER TIP

This important point about Eugenics should have been developed to show how the subject might lead German students to believe it was acceptable to mistreat 'inferior' races.

EXAMINER TIP

This paragraph explains the purpose of the Hitler Youth well. It would be helpful if the student gave some assessment of its success. Why did the Nazis pass Youth Laws in 1936 and 1939?

OVERALL COMMENT

This answer would achieve Level 3 for its detailed knowledge of the way the school curriculum changed and the activities of the Hitler Youth. It could achieve Level 4 if it recognised that there were different effects on different groups of students who responded in different ways at different times. Some resented the Hitler Youth or had different experiences in cities or in Church youth groups. The biggest impact of these changes would have been on family life.

OVER TO YOU

1   How would you improve the sample answer?

2   Now it's time for you to have a go at planning and writing an answer to this question. Spend about 10 minutes on your answer.

3   Now check your answer. Did you do the following?

☐   Did you name at least two ways in which young people were affected by Nazi policies?

☐   For each way, did you add a few details based on your own knowledge (facts) and understanding to explain why it had an impact?

Go back to pages 40–41 of this Revision Guide to refresh your memory of the different ways young people were affected by Nazi policies.

EXAMINER TIP

Try to refer to what the Nazis wanted to achieve through their youth policies.

The 'bullet points' question

EXAM QUESTION

6   Which of the following had the greater impact on the German people:
   • the Treaty of Versailles
   • the hyperinflation crisis of 1923?
   Explain your answer with reference to both events.   **12 marks**

EXAMINER TIP

The aim of the bullet points question is to get you to show that you know about the reasons, events and consequences of the period in German history that you have studied. You might be asked to focus on results, impacts or causes. This particular question focuses on two events in the early years of the Weimar period. You will also have to reach a judgement (conclusion) that relates to the question.

Sample student answer

The Treaty of Versailles had a major impact on the German people. For a start, it was humiliating because they were blamed for starting a war they felt they didn't start. Also, lots of Germans hated the Treaty because they felt that they hadn't actually lost the war – German soldiers were still based in France and Belgium, on foreign soil, when the war ended, for example. The Treaty of Versailles punished Germany in all sorts of ways. As well as blaming Germany, the country had to reduce their army to 100,000 soldiers, they had to have a small navy and no submarines, tanks or airforce. As well as this being humiliating because Germany had once been such a great military power, it also left them weak and vulnerable against attack. They also lost land and colonies which had an economic impact because it meant that the land and the factories could not make money for the country. Also, they had to pay £6.6 billion in reparations to the winning countries. This was on top of the money they would need to spend to get Germany back on its feet – so the Treaty of Versailles ruined Germany as a military power and an economic force.

The hyperinflation crisis of 1923 also had a great impact on the German people. When Germany couldn't pay the reparations they owed, France sent troops to a richer area of Germany called the Ruhr. This area was very industrial and produced iron so France wanted to get its money by taking the iron. Germans in the area went on strike to stop the French getting these resources, which meant that Germany had even less money as they were no longer making ANY money from the Ruhr. To try and sort out the money problem, and pay the striking workers, the government started to print lots of money until eventually there was so much money around that it became worthless. Soon prices were rising by millions every day.

The impact of hyperinflation was huge. People with savings in the bank were really badly affected. They might have saved all their lives to get 1000 marks in the bank and now this wouldn't even buy them a loaf of bread. Old people who lived on fixed pensions found their money wouldn't buy them what they needed any more and many small businesses collapsed as normal trade became impossible because of the daily price changes. Not surprisingly, many Germans blamed the government for the mess, because it was their decision to call a strike in the Ruhr and then to print so much money.

In conclusion, I think it was the Treaty of Versailles that had the greatest impact.

EXAMINER TIP

This answer goes into detail about the impact of the Treaty of Versailles.

EXAMINER TIP

This paragraph shows good understanding of hyperinflation's **impact** on Germans. Also, the student has not wasted time by writing about things that are not related to the bullet points: the Treaty of Versailles and the hyperinflation crisis of 1923.

EXAMINER TIP

This conclusion is weak. The question asks which had the *greater* impact. The student needs to give reasons why they thought the Treaty of Versailles had greater impact than the hyperinflation crisis.

OVERALL COMMENT

This answer would achieve Level 3. A conclusion similar to the following would have helped the answer achieve a Level 4:

I think that the Treaty of Versailles had the greater impact because Germany had struggled through four years of war, which touched all families, and the civilian population suffered shortages. All Germans would have felt the dishonour, anger and hatred of the Treaty. The hyperinflation lasted for less time than the sense of injustice caused by the Treaty.

OVER TO YOU

1   Read the sample answer again, but this time highlight in different colours where it mentions:

- the impact that the Treaty of Versailles had on the German people

- the impact that the hyperinflation crisis of 1923 had on the German people.

Underline the sentences where the student gives reasons why they think one of the bullet points made a greater impact on the German people.

2   Have a go at writing your own rough essay plan to the question. You only have 15 minutes on this question, so don't spend more than four minutes creating the rough plan. Check your plan.

☐ Did you plan what you will say for each of the two bullet points?

☐ Did you come to a quick decision (judgement) about whether hyperinflation or the Treaty of Versailles had a greater impact on Germans?

☐ Did you note down one or two reasons **why** one of those bullets had a greater impact? (Remember, explaining why you came to your conclusion would help you get higher marks.)

☐ Did you manage to complete your plan within four minutes?

3   Use your essay plan to answer this question. You may want to review pages 16—19 to refresh your knowledge on the Treaty of Versailles and the hyperinflation crisis, and their impacts on Germans.

The answers provided here are examples, based on the information provided in the Recap sections of this Revision Guide. There may be other factors which are relevant to each question, and you should draw on as much of your own knowledge as possible to give detailed and precise answers. There are also many ways of answering exam questions (for example, of structuring an essay). However, these exemplar answers should provide a good starting point.

Chapter 1 Page 13
DESCRIBE

a
- Kaiser: the German emperor
- Bundesrat: group made up of German state representatives who supported the Kaiser
- Reichstag: the main, elected German parliament
- Militarism: belief that a country should maintain a strong armed forces and be prepared to use it aggressively
- Socialism: system of government which supports democracy and greater government involvement in the economy and society
- Navy Laws: series of laws introduced from 1898 to 1912 that expanded the size of the navy

b German workers unhappy with pay and conditions – they joined trade unions, went on more strikes; increase in support for socialism, which threatened the status and power of the upper classes; high debts as a result of expansion of army and navy; taxes increased which made workers even more unhappy

c Answer might include:
- Increase in popularity of the SPD that opposed the privileges of the Kaiser and his inner circle.
- Increase in trade union membership – more power to the workers.
- Debt as a result of the increase in military spending – increased taxes upset Germans, and borrowed money would need to be paid back.
- Rise of extreme socialism was a direct threat to the Kaiser's power and status.

Chapter 2 Page 15
IN WHAT WAYS

a Words could include patriotism, protest, shortages, instability, division, bankrupt, mutiny, abdication, revolution, and defeat.

b Answers might include:
- Changed happened gradually over time.
- War was greeted with great enthusiasm at first.
- Rationing had started as early as 1915.
- War weariness/discontent from 1915.

- British blockade reduced imports and food shortages were a problem.
- Prices rose and by 1918 food shortages were severe.
- People's loyalty was tested and because news of military failures filtered through, discontent rose. Support for socialism increased, especially because of news of the Bolshevik Revolution in Russia.

DESCRIBE

a
- Ebert declared that Germany would be a democratic republic and arranged for elections for a new Parliament.
- Spartacists seized power in Berlin.
- Ebert sent the Free Corps to attack the Spartacists.
- The Free Corps recaptured buildings and arrested Spartacist leaders.
- Elections were held; Ebert became the new German President.
- During the revolt, politicians had met in Weimar. They created the Weimar Constitution and Weimar Republic.

b A left-wing, communist group that wanted Germany to be run by small councils of soldiers and workers, not by a large parliament.

c
- Strengths
  - Elections were held regularly.
  - All Germans had equal rights, including the right to vote.
  - All men and women over the age of 20 could vote by proportional representation.
- Weaknesses
  - Proportional representation meant that it was difficult for one party to get a majority.
  - Many groups (including older army generals and upper-class families) didn't like this new democratic system of governing.
  - The new system of government was linked to the 'November Criminals'.

d Weaknesses might include two of the following:
- Proportional representation meant that lots of different political parties were able to win some seats in the Reichstag, but it was difficult for one party to get a majority – law-making was very slow.
- Some groups didn't like new democratic system of governing. Some older army generals, judges, upper-class families, rich factory owners and university professors longed for the 'good old days' when the Kaiser ruled Germany.
- New system of government and the politicians who created it were linked to

Germany's defeat at the end of the First World War. Some Germans called these politicians 'November Criminals'.
- The constitution contained Article 48 which meant that laws could be passed without the Reichstag by order of the President.

Page 17
INTERPRETATION ANALYSIS

a List might include:
- The war was Germany's fault, so Germany must pay for the costs of the war.
- Germany should only have a small army, navy, and no submarines, tanks or air force.
- Large areas of German land to be used to create new countries (such as Poland and Czechoslovakia).
- Germany must never unite with Austria.
- No German soldiers should enter the Rhineland.

b Answer might include:
- The Treaty took away large areas of land, which meant losing people, factories, farms and mines. They had to pay a large amount of money to the winners.
- They were ordered to sign the Treaty, without discussion. They called it a *diktat* – a dictated peace.
- Many Germans felt that politicians had betrayed the country by asking for a ceasefire.
- They felt humiliated by loss of territory and reduction of military.

c
- Hitler blames all of Germany's later problems (political and economic) on the Treaty.
- You should state and justify your own opinion.

Page 19
IN WHAT WAYS

a Flow chart should include:
- French and Belgian troops invaded the Ruhr in response to the German government's failure to pay reparations.
- German workers were ordered to go on strike in the Ruhr, but were still paid.
- The German government printed lots of money to pay striking workers and its debts to France and Belgium.
- As workers spent money in the shops, shopkeepers began to put up their prices.
- The German government printed even more money, so shops raised their prices again.
- Soon prices were inflating so fast that it became known as hyperinflation.

b Answer might include:

- People with bank savings lost their money.
- Elderly people on fixed pensions found their income wouldn't buy them what they needed any more.
- Many small businesses collapsed as normal trade became impossible because of the daily price changes.
- However, people who had borrowed money found it very easy to pay off their debts.

Chapter 3 Page 21

BULLET POINTS

a Your brief explanation of the key individuals should show how they relate to the content of the chapter. For example, Wolfgang Kapp was a former politician and journalist who, helped by around 5000 Free Corps members, briefly took control of Berlin in March 1920. He aimed to take over the whole country, make the army strong again, and recover the lands Germany had lost in the Treaty of Versailles.

b The rating will be an individual choice, but you should be able to justify it.

c A good answer would give a complex explanation of both bullet points in two paragraphs, leading to a concluding paragraph in which the relative merits of each bullet point are discussed. You should name and explain examples of both right-wing and left-wing threats and the part they played in making the Weimar Republic unstable. Left-wing risings: Spartacists (January 1919); communist riots (March 1919); Ruhr rising (21 March 1920). Right-wing risings: Kapp Putsch (13 March 1920); assassinations (1920–22); Munich Putsch (November 1923).

INTERPRETATION ANALYSIS

Answer might include:

a The source suggests Hitler was cowardly and not keen to begin the revolt because he wanted to make himself scarce. It says that Hitler threw himself on the ground when the shooting started, hurt his arm and then got into his car and drove off.

b Reasons might include: he was an opponent of the Nazis and had many articles and books banned by them. As a result he may have been critical of the Nazis and keen to show them in a negative light.

c Answer might conclude that it is difficult to know exactly what happened because people who were there all have their own views and opinions on Hitler and the Nazis and this may influence their views of the event. Also, many of the people involved may now be dead, or may struggle to remember the details of something that happened such a long time ago or in a situation as full of confusion as a firefight.

Page 23

IN WHAT WAYS

a Stresemann was briefly Chancellor in 1923 but is best known as Germany's Foreign Minster from 1924 until his death in 1929; seen as a great help to Germany during crisis of 1920s.

b

- Hyperinflation: Policy – Stopped printing of old paper money and replaced it with the Rentenmark – a new, stable currency.
- French and Belgian occupation of the Ruhr: Policy – Met with US Vice President Dawes and arranged for the USA to lend money to Germany; Germany could now begin to pay what they owed and French and Belgian troops left the Ruhr.
- Poor relationship with other countries: Policy – In 1925 Germany signed the Locarno Pact with Britain, France, Belgium and Italy, promising to never invade each other; in 1926 Germany joined the League of Nations; in 1928 Germany signed the Kellogg-Briand Pact – participating countries agreed never to go to war, unless to defend themselves.

You should make your own judgements, using evidence to support them.

c Answer should include:

- He stopped the printing of banknotes and replaced the worthless notes with the Rentenmark, ending hyperinflation. However, people who had lost all their savings never got their money back, and blamed Stresemann and his government.
- The Dawes Plan, arranged by Stresemann, meant reparations payments could be resumed and French and Belgian troops left the Ruhr. US money from the plan was used to build new factories, houses, schools and roads. This meant more jobs, with Germans earning more money. The Young Plan of 1929 saw reparation payments reduced.
- Germans felt safer as a result of the 1925 Locarno Pact. In 1928, Germany signed the Kellogg-Briand Pact. The participating countries agreed never to go to war, unless in self-defence.
- Germany regained its international status, joining the League of Nations in 1926. Germany's membership demonstrated acceptance of the Treaty and a desire to be at peace.

DESCRIBE

a A way of thinking, behaving or working that exists in a place, country or organisation.

b Answer might include:

- The 1920s were a 'golden age' for German artists, writers, poets and performers, who became known for their creativity and innovation.
- Before the war, the Kaiser kept tight control of all types of entertainment, but the controls were removed in Weimar Germany. As a result there was a new sense of freedom and many people decided to experiment with new ideas and try new things.
- For example, Germany became a centre for new plays, operas and theatre. Musicians performed vulgar songs, about politicians, that would have been banned under the Kaiser. Berlin was famous for its nightclubs with live bands that played American jazz.

Chapter 4 Page 25

DESCRIBE

a List might include: unemployment, poverty, hardship, factory closures, bank failure, Wall Street Crash, hopelessness, etc.

b List might include: unhappiness with inability of Weimar politicians to deal with the crisis; frustration with democratic system; Nazi promises of work; appeal of Hitler – charismatic, good leadership qualities; fear or hatred of communism/ left-wingers.

You should identify two of the words or phrases that you wrote in answer to the first task and add detail. For example, when the Americans stopped buying German-made goods, many German factories went bankrupt. As a result, millions lost their jobs. People were soon living on the streets – jobless, hungry and angry at their political leaders who they blamed for their problems.

INTERPRETATION ANALYSIS

Answer might include:

a Kehrl was frustrated with the Weimar politicians and impressed with the Nazi party promises to get Germany out of its difficulties. He was taken by their promise to solve unemployment and build up agricultural life – and do it quickly. He felt they could deal with the hopeless situation Germany was in.

b Answer might include that Kehrl was critical of how Weimar politicians were pulling in different directions rather than together, arguing over policy matters.

Page 27

DESCRIBE

a Table might include the following points:

- The Depression: People felt the Weimar government was doing little to deal with it; Hitler offered a solution
- Discontent with Weimar government: Weimar democracy was seen as failing, Germany still in a mess, Weimar politicians had no solutions;

Weaknesses of the constitution – too many parties meant making clear decisions was nearly impossible
- Fear of communism: Middle/upper classes feared a communist takeover like in Russia, Hitler promised to fight communism from the start; He sent his own private army, the Stormtroopers (SA), to fight with communist gangs
- Appeal of Hitler: Charismatic speaker; Great propagandist – use of new media and technology (radio, aeroplanes, etc.) spread Nazi message
- Nazi Party structure and methods: Nazis appeared the most organised and disciplined group in the country – offices set up all over Germany to recruit more loyal followers; Nazis promoted as a party that might restore Germany's greatness

b There will be a variety of different reasons, but a good answer should reference all of them as a combination of reasons.

c Answer should cover in detail two of the reasons listed in the chart.

BULLET POINTS

a Mind-map should pull together reasons for the Nazis' popularity from across the chapter.

b You might write about each of these factors in isolation and then try to make a link between the two: for example, how the Nazis were expert propagandists and used the Depression in their posters and leaflets. Hitler said that the impact of the Depression was proof that Weimar democracy had failed and that he offered a solution.

You might decide to favour one side: for example, the Depression helped the Nazis more than the methods. Before the onset of the Depression, the Nazis were using many of the methods but were still only the eighth most popular party. However, by 1930, after the Depression had hit Germany hard, the Nazis had 107 seats in the Reichstag from a low of 12 in 1928.

Chapter 5 Page 29
DESCRIBE

a Answers should be similar to:
- Majority: over half the votes or politicians in a parliament
- coalition government: when two or more political parties combine to rule
- Article 48: part of the Weimar Constitution that gave the President the right to rule in a time of crisis without requiring the support of the Reichstag

b Answer might include: Hindenburg refused to give Hitler the Chancellor's job to begin with because he thought the Nazis were a disruptive party so he used his emergency powers to give the job to a number of other men, including von Papen and von Schleicher. Eventually, Hindenburg tried to limit Hitler's power by appointing von Papen as Vice

Chancellor and only allowing Hitler to have two other Nazis in the cabinet.

BULLET POINTS

a Timeline should include details from the 1930 Reichstag election and the two Reichstag elections of 1932 as well as the presidential election of March 1932. You should also include the changes of Chancellor at various stages.

b A good answer might explain the part played by both the Depression and the political factors that interlinked to cause an increase in Nazi electoral support, to the point where Hitler had significant seats in the Reichstag and was invited to be Chancellor. The interplay of economic depression with the inability of Weimar governments to deal with unemployment led to the sudden appeal of extremists. Therefore, the reason why Hitler was appointed Chancellor of Germany in 1933 was because he led the largest party in the Reichstag. Von Papen was keen, with Hindenburg, to take advantage of this Nazi popularity but wanted to ensure that Hitler stayed under his control so that he could make the real decisions.

Chapter 6 Page 31
IN WHAT WAYS

a The key dates are: 27 February 1933; 28 February 1933; 23 March 1933; 7 April 1933; 2 May 1933; 14 July 1933; 2 August 1934. You should describe what happened and how it helped Hitler consolidate his power. For example: On 27 February 1933 the Reichstag burned down. Hitler went to Hindenburg and used the fire as 'evidence' of a communist plot. He tried to get Hindenburg to ban the communist party, which would mean that ordinary Germans could not be communists or vote for a political party that was opposed to the Nazis. This was one of Hitler's first steps in getting rid of his opposition.

b
- Use of law – In March 1933 Hitler used a new law (the 'Decree for the Protection of the People and the State') to ban leading communists. This meant that there was less political opposition on his road to dictatorship.
- Political scheming – On 23 March 1933, politicians in another political party, the Centre Party, were persuaded to join the Nazis. This meant that Hitler now had the majority he wanted and could introduce new laws as he saw fit.
- Bullying and aggression – In February 1933, after arranging another election, Hitler used the police and SA to intimidate people into voting for him.
- Chance and opportunism – On 27 February the Reichstag building burned down. Hitler used this opportunity to blame the communists,

which led him to pressure the President to pass an emergency 'Protection Law'.

c Answer might reference: Weimar Constitution and the fact that it guaranteed political and social freedoms; Hitler's gradual erosion of these freedoms by introducing laws to ban particular groups (trade unions, communist party, other political parties); intimidation and bullying of other parties such as the Centre Party, including locking up political opponents and banning their newspapers.

Page 32
DESCRIBE

a Answers should be similar to:
- Ernst Rohm: leader of the SA
- The SA: Hitler's brown-shirted supporters who were employed to beat up opponents and guard meetings
- The SS: led by Heinrich Himmler, suppressed Hitler's political opponents and persecuted Jews

b Create your own test.

c Answers might include any of these consequences:
- Hitler's main political opponents and threats from within the Nazi Party were dead. Showed Hitler's ruthlessness and that he was happy to operate above the law.
- The SS emerged as the group now responsible for Hitler's security, not the SA.
- Hitler made the army swear a personal oath of loyalty to him. The army leaders agreed to stay out of politics and serve Hitler.
- Hitler promised to spend large sums of money to make Germany a great military power once more.
- There was now no person or thing within Germany that had the power to oppose him as Führer.

Page 33
INTERPRETATION ANALYSIS

a Spider diagram might include:
- Who? Ernst Rohm and other SA leaders killed. Over next few days around 400 political opponents were also executed by SS assassination squad.
- What? Meeting arranged between Hitler and SA leaders at a hotel on 30 June 1934. Shortly before dawn, Hitler and the SS squad stormed into the hotel and arrested SA chief Rohm and other SA leaders.
- When? 30 June 1934, and others executed in the days that followed.
- Where? Hotel in Bavaria, southern Germany.
- Why? SA and Rohm viewed as a threat. The SA were unemployed, violent thugs loyal to Rohm. Hitler felt Rohm was becoming too powerful – already more SA members than German army. Rohm also

wanted to merge the SA with the army, with both under his control. This alarmed Hitler, as well as the army leaders.

- Impact? Hitler's main political opponents and threats from within Nazi Party were dead. Showed Hitler's ruthlessness and that he was happy to operate above the law. SS emerged as the group now responsible for Hitler's security, not the SA. Hitler then made the army swear a personal oath of loyalty to him.

b Answers might include:

1 According to the report in Interpretation A, Rohm was critical of the army leadership (and his 'former' friend Hitler) and believed that the SA, under his leadership, would replace the army. This would be a threat to Hitler because he needed the army's support for his plans for war. The army consisted of trained professional soldiers but the generals in particular had the strategic and tactical know-how to fight battles. Rohm was alienating them. However, Interpretation B suggests simply that the SA were a threat because they were out of control — beyond the law.

2 Interpretation A describes an overheard conversation that was remembered possibly four or five years later, and written in the safety of the United States, by a former Nazi during a time of war. All of these circumstances would affect the author's view. Interpretation B comes from an American non-Nazi, who was highly connected and could speak directly to a government minister. He also reported a conversation, and wrote about it six or seven years later, when America was at war with Nazi Germany. All of these things could have affected the author's view. For example, he may have wished to show the Nazis in a poor light to justify being at war with them.

3 If Interpretation A is accurate then Hitler's plans for expansion in the east, Lebensraum, overturning Versailles, rearming, and uniting German-speaking peoples would be placed in jeopardy as the army high command would be vital. However, Interpretation B shows the threat thousands of Brownshirts could pose to Nazi government. Hitler had the SS to control the SA and secure his long-term control and plans.

Chapter 7 Page 35

IN WHAT WAYS

a Write your own revision cards.

b Answers could include:
- Yes: Hardworking German workers were rewarded through Strength through Joy; Nazis tried to improve working

environment by installing better lighting, safety equipment, new washrooms
- No: Some holidays, such as cruises around Italy or skiing in Switzerland, were still too expensive for most working-class Germans; Food cost more because Germany was trying to be self-sufficient but couldn't produce as much food [en-rule] shopkeepers charged more because of high demand

c Answer might include: how trade unions were replaced, strikes were made illegal, workers needed permission to leave jobs. However, the Nazis promised to protect workers' rights and improve conditions by running two schemes to improve Germans' lives: SDA (tried to improve workplace by installing better lighting, safety equipment, and sports facilities) and KDF (organised leisure activities to encourage hard work; reward scheme with cheap holidays, theatre trips and football match tickets). Answer might also reference the way the Nazis created work schemes to fight unemployment and created the National Labour Service (RAD) for all men aged between 18 and 25.

Page 37

IN WHAT WAYS

a When a country operates without external assistance or international trade

b Spider diagram should include: German scientists found ways to make petrol from coal, artificial wool and cotton from pulped wood, make-up from flour, and coffee from acorns.

c Answer might include: the focus was on the increased production of weaponry and the materials associated with it (oil, steel, etc.); move towards self-sufficiency could mean that the Nazis knew that they did not have to rely on imports from future enemies — or across seas that may become theatres of war.

INTERPRETATION ANALYSIS

a Minister of Economics until 1936, dismissed from the government completely in 1943.

b Folly, incompetence, amateur, exploited, nonsense

c Schacht saw Goering as a rival, who replaced him when he was sacked; Goering was not an economist, but one of the 'rough' Nazis.

Page 39

DESCRIBE

a Rationing
- Definition/explanation: As a result of food shortages, the government limited the amount of food and goods that people could buy
- Impact: Some Germans faced hardship

as they could not get the goods they needed; impact on morale; a sign that the war was not going well

Total War
- Definition/explanation: When everything is focused on making weapons and growing food for soldiers; anything that doesn't contribute to the war is stopped
- Impact: Everyday life changed: beer halls (pubs), dance halls and sweet shops were closed; factories stayed open longer and brought people into the war who would not normally be involved (eg. women)

Labour shortages
- Definition/explanation: When there are not enough people to do the jobs required.
- Impact: Women drafted in to work in factories; around seven million foreign workers brought in to work as slave labour.

Bombing
- Definition/explanation: The aeroplane bombing attacks from 1942 as Britain and America began bombing German cities
- Impact: As well as the human cost in lives, there was no electricity, water or transport in many German cities; thousands lost their homes

Bombing
- Definition/explanation: People who leave their homes to move to safer places
- Impact: Ordinary Germans had to leave their homes; people flooded into other areas; morale declined

b Answer should contain a detailed description of how two of the following had an impact on German citizens: rationing, Total War, labour shortages, bombing, refugees.

INTERPRETATION ANALYSIS

a
- Nazi, Armaments Minister, prepared Germany for Total War.
- He said air raid warnings went on for weeks, with only occasional nights without them when bad weather stopped enemy raids, but people's morale was not affected.
- Reasons include: he was lying when interviewed; or it was actually high; or he was ashamed that he had failed to protect the German people.

Chapter 8 Page 41

DESCRIBE

a
- German Teachers League – a Nazi organisation to which all teachers had to belong. Teachers had to teach what the

Nazis wanted, or be sacked.

- Eugenics – Race Studies, a school subject that taught students that the Aryan race was superior to others.
- Hitler Youth Organisation – a series of youth groups for young Germans that educated and trained them in Nazi principles.
- Napolas – special academies that trained potential Nazi leaders.

b Answer should be a detailed description of two methods the Hitler Youth used to control the lives of young people, and the Nazis' use of propaganda:

- Boys going to Hitler Youth meetings several times a week after school, and to special weekend camps every month. Learning how to march, fight with knives, fire a gun, and keep themselves fit.
- Emphasis for girls on how to keep fit, cook good meals and care for babies, to prepare for motherhood. Girls also went on tough marches and attended weekend camps.
- School textbooks contained Nazi propaganda and beliefs, and university courses were altered to reflect Nazi doctrine.

INTERPRETATION ANALYSIS

a Mind-map might include the following:

Why? branch

- If young people were brought up to believe in Nazi ideas, they would grow up to be good Nazis who would never rebel against the regime.
- Hitler believed that young children who learned to idolise him would continue to admire and fight for him for the rest of their lives.
- The Hitler Youth Organisation prepared boys for future role as soldiers and girls for roles as wives and mothers.

How? branch

- Schools
  - Teachers joined German Teachers League – taught what the Nazis wanted or were sacked.
  - Textbooks rewritten to reflect Nazi beliefs.
  - Students taught that Aryan race was superior to others.
  - Future Nazi leaders sent to special academies known as 'Napolas' (National Political Educational Institutions) or 'Adolf Hitler Schools'.
- Universities
  - Courses changed to reflect Nazi beliefs.
  - All students had to train as soldiers for a month each year.
  - Top professors hand-picked by the Nazis.
- Hitler Youth Organisation
  - All other youth groups banned

  - Controlled all sports facilities and youth competitions
  - Membership made compulsory in 1939
  - German boys
    - Hitler Youth meetings several times a week after school
    - Learned to march, fight with knives, fire a gun, keep fit
    - Emphasis on competition, struggle, heroism and leadership
  - German girls
    - Tough marches, attended weekend camps
    - Learned how to keep fit, cook meals and look after babies

b Answer might include:

- Progressive, more forward-thinking, even 'better' teachers left. Some teachers who joined had been reprimanded/censored and had to conform now. Some, however, didn't work in a school again, showing the power/far-reaching consequences of Nazi policies towards teachers. Nazis allowed some teachers to work in their SA uniform, showing that the education system and the state were closely linked.
- Her background may colour her opinion – working class, left-wing, so naturally opposed to the right/fascists. Her father was a victim of the SA, so she may hate them as a result.

Page 43

DESCRIBE

a

- The three Ks – Nazi focus for women: Kinder (children), Kirche (church), Küche (cooking).
- Motherhood Medals – awarded to women with the most children; mothers with eight children received the 'Gold Cross'.
- German Women's League – coordinated all adult women's groups; representatives gave advice on cooking, childcare and diet.
- Sterilisation policy – 'Law for the Prevention of Diseased Offspring' allowed forcible sterilisation of women with a history of mental illness, hereditary diseases or anti-social behaviour.

b Answer should describe in detail two Nazi policies. For example, there was an effort by the Nazis to increase the birth rate, which had declined in the Weimar period – contraception and abortion were banned and generous loans were given to newly married couples to encourage them to have children. The Motherhood Medal was awarded to women with the most children. Mothers with eight children received the 'Gold Cross'.

BULLET POINTS

a Chart might include the following:

Women before the Nazis

- Many rights and freedoms that women in other countries did not have; e.g. right to vote, equal pay.
- Many women attended university and became lawyers and doctors.
- Birth rate in decline.

Nazi beliefs about the role of women

- Worried about declining birth rate – low birth rate and a lower population didn't fit with their plans to expand Germany's territory and settle Germans in other areas of Europe.
- Women's patriotic duty to stay at home, have lots of children and support their husbands.
- Three Ks – Kinder, Kirche and Küche (children, church and cooking).

Nazi policies relating to women

- Female doctors, teachers, lawyers and judges were sacked.
- Women banned from smoking because it was 'unladylike'.
- Loans given to newly-weds to encourage them to have children.
- Banned contraception and abortion.
- Motherhood Medal awarded to women with the most children.

Impact of Nazi policies

- Thousands of women prevented from following their chosen career path.
- Birth rate increased.
- When the war started, the Nazis needed women back at work because more men were joining the army.

b A good answer would describe changes to young Germans' school lives as well as their leisure hours. This could be further differentiated by gender and the Nazi expectations of boys and girls. Some comment should be made about German women's expectations with regard to work and family.

You should also identify ways in which these expectations changed during the time of Nazi control. For example, young people who entered the Hitler Youth in 1933–34 were part of a physical activity-based, fun, exciting organisation. By 1938–39 the former Hitler Youth members had been drafted into the army and the Hitler Youth was a much more military, competitive and demanding organisation. Women were initially encouraged to give up work to look after the home and have babies. But by 1938, as men joined the armed forces, women were expected to work in factories to produce munitions for the war effort.

Page 45

DESCRIBE

a Differences might include:

- Nazis thought strength and violence

were glorious, whereas Christians believe in love and forgiveness.
- Nazis hated the weak and vulnerable, while Christians believe in helping the weak and vulnerable.
- Nazis believed that some races were better than others but Christians believe all people are equal in God's eyes.
- Nazis saw Hitler as a God-like figure, but Christians believe in God and the teachings of Jesus Christ.

Similarities might include:
- A belief in marriage, the family and moral values.
- Hitler was opposed to communism. Christians disapproved of communism as it was anti-religious.

b Answer might include:
- Some Christians supported Nazi policy because the Nazis believed in the importance of marriage, the family and moral values. Most Christians believe in the importance of these too. Hitler had sworn to destroy communism. This appealed to Christians because communism was anti-religious.
- At first Hitler cooperated with Catholic leaders and they agreed not to interfere with each other's work. However, soon Catholic priests were harassed and arrested, and Catholic youth clubs and schools were closed down. In 1937, the Pope issued his 'With Burning Anxiety' statement. This said that the Nazis were 'hostile to Christ and his Church'. In August 1941, Catholic Archbishop Galen openly criticised the Nazis. He was put under house arrest until the end of the war.
- Some Protestants, known as 'German Christians', wanted to see their Church under Nazi control. Their leader (Ludwig Müller) became the first Reich Bishop in September 1933. They wore Nazi uniforms and used the slogan 'the swastika on our chests and the Cross in our hearts'.

BULLET POINTS

a Create your own flashcards.

b A good answer would explain that older women would have a different experience from that of younger women. Women who had been through the Nazi education system may have been influenced to support the Nazis more and accept their role as the Nazis saw it. Older women who had lived through the Depression may have been grateful for the stability and prosperity that the Nazis brought. However, older women with sons may not have been pleased with the prospect of them joining the armed forces.

A good answer would also break down

'Christians' into further groups – Roman Catholics and Protestants, which could be broken down further into 'German Christians' and the Confessional Church – and detail their treatment.

Page 47

INTERPRETATION ANALYSIS

a Write your own definitions.

b Create your own timeline, which might start in March 1933: Jewish lawyers, judges, teachers (and later, doctors) were sacked.

Chapter 9 Page 49

DESCRIBE

a A country where the police and other organisations linked to the police (such as the courts) are very powerful and act on behalf of the government.

b
- Gestapo: part of the SS and Nazi Germany's secret police force, created by Herman Goering in 1933 and controlled by Heinrich Himmler
- Concentration camp: camp in which people are held under harsh conditions and without the freedoms of the rest of society
- The SS: led by Heinrich Himmler, suppressed Hitler's political opponents and persecuted Jews

c Answer should focus on the way that the Nazis used two of the following: regular police and the law courts, Gestapo, concentration camps and the SS.

INTERPRETATION ANALYSIS

a Roberts thinks that German attitude to the Jews was that they were a threat. He says that Germans felt that the persecution was a good thing, and didn't argue against it – they thought young people should be taught about the danger that the Jews posed. Roberts seems surprised that there was little opposition to this view.

b Roberts was an intelligent man who had travelled widely in Germany, met and listened to Nazi leaders speaking at rallies, and talked to the Germans who attended them. He had lots of evidence to support these views. As an Australian, he would have previously lived in a democracy free from such persecution.

c Roberts's views are convincing because otherwise how would the Nazis have got away with persecuting Jews from the moment they came to power in 1933. The Nazis did change the school curriculum to make it anti-Semitic and there was anti-Semitic literature. However, Roberts is writing to warn people about Nazi actions against the Jews. If Germans did not like the anti-Semitic propaganda they could ignore it and they might be unwilling to share this dislike with a stranger like Roberts, who

could inform on them to the Nazis.

Page 51

DESCRIBE

a Make your own flashcards. One example might be for 'Film'. On the reverse: 'The Nazis used films to get across their views and ideas. At the cinema Germans would only see films that showed the Nazis in a good light.'

b List should include: censorship laws; propaganda; harsh penalties for listening to foreign radio stations; ban on critical books, films, articles and jokes; fear and intimidation.

c Answer should summarise the idea of Nazi control of information – they ensured their own messages reached the population while preventing alternative messages from being heard – and then go into detail on two examples. For example: on the radio, all radio stations were under Nazi control – they broadcast only Nazi ideas. Cheap radios were produced that could only tune in to Nazi-controlled stations. Loudspeakers were placed in the streets, in factories and in cafes to air radio broadcasts. There were negative news stories about Germany's 'enemies'. Newspapers that didn't comply were closed down.

INTERPRETATION ANALYSIS

a Answer might include:
- Negative stories about Germany's 'enemies'.
- Radio stations put across only Nazi ideas.
- Writers were forced to write books, plays and songs that praised Hitler and the Nazis.

b The writer makes the point that it's hard for people to understand if they haven't lived in a dictatorship – when you keep hearing the same message, and don't hear any other messages, it's very difficult to think independently because you have no other views to compare things to in order to make your own decisions.

Page 53

DESCRIBE

a
- The Chamber of Culture – an organisation set up by the Nazis and controlled by Joseph Goebbels that aimed to make sure that cultural activities reflected Nazi ideas.
- The Militant League for German Culture – a group set up in the Weimar period that protested against some of the more 'modern' plays and films during the 1920s.
- The 'Bauhaus' movement – an important architectural and design development in Weimar Germany that favoured practical, modern buildings and objects.

b Answer could include:

- Nazi supporters such as Alfred Hugenberg owned film studios, so the Nazis had a direct influence on how films were made. Goebbels read and approved all film scripts. All films had to carry a pro-Nazi message. News reports of Nazi achievements were always shown before the main film. Books classed as 'Un-German' or those by Jewish authors were removed from libraries and bookshops and sometimes burned. Goebbels encouraged books about race, the glory of war and the brilliance of the Nazis.

BULLET POINTS

a Chart might include:

- **Cinema:** How changed? Goebbels made sure he read and approved all film scripts; All films had to carry a pro-Nazi message. Why changed? To get across Nazi views; To suppress other views
- **Music:** How changed? Marching music, old folk songs and classical music by German and Austrian composers such as Bach, Beethoven, Mozart and Wagner were encouraged; Some music that was popular in Weimar Germany was banned. Why changed? To encourage patriotism, music was militaristic, and German/Austrian jazz was banned because of 'inferior' origins
- **Theatre:** How changed? Plays should mainly focus on German history and politics; Cabaret clubs were closed down. Why changed? Plays were to focus on German history and military for propaganda purposes; Cabarets were banned because they were seen as places where songs about sex and politics were common
- **Literature:** How changed? List of banned books was created; Some books were gathered and burned; Books about race, the glory of war and the brilliance of the Nazis were encouraged; Some popular books written in Weimar Germany were banned, e.g. *All Quiet on the Western Front*. Why changed? To get across Nazi views; To suppress other views
- **Art:** How changed? Nazis encouraged art that was simple and clearly understandable, showing healthy, heroic German figures and family scenes of happy, strong 'pure' Germans; Examples of modern 'degenerate' art were banned and even burned. Why changed? To get across Nazi views on the family, ideal German, etc.; To suppress other views
- **Design:** How changed? Big, public buildings like libraries, government buildings and parade grounds were built – huge, stone structures, often copies of buildings from ancient Greece or Rome; The 'Bauhaus' movement was closed down in 1933. Why changed? New buildings to show the power of the Nazi movement; Hitler didn't approve of modern design
- **Sport:** How changed? Success in sport was used to promote the Nazi regime; The Olympic Games, held in Berlin in 1936, were used for propaganda. Why changed? Health and fitness important to Nazis – soldiers and mothers needed to be fit and healthy; Olympics used to promote Nazi ideals

b The police state was made up of Nazi-run organisations that checked up on people's behaviour, e.g. Gestapo and SS, and the courts were controlled by the Nazis too, with the power to send people to concentration camps. People knew that this system existed, which created a climate of fear in which society policed itself and generated armies of informers.

The role of propaganda was to educate people on how to think and behave while also preventing them from hearing opposing views. Media control was vital. Film and radio were the two most current and immediate media and the Nazis were able to control the ideas and values that were broadcast. It was very difficult for Germans to decide how to resist or oppose this propaganda. Although it was easier for older people who had previous knowledge to set against the propaganda, many were grateful for Hitler and the Nazis' resurrection of Germany, having lived through the Depression.

A summary paragraph might express the opinion that fear of the consequences from the police state made people accept propaganda messages.

INTERPRETATION ANALYSIS

a Lochner wrote that the 'civilised' world was shocked when the Nazis burned books, which means that he thinks members of the Nazi regime are not part of the 'civilised' world'. He also appears to make a sarcastic reference to the Minister for Propaganda – Goebbels – as someone who is acting with 'supreme wisdom' because Lochner thinks this is a stupid act.

b Lochner was an eyewitness to the events as he lived in Germany at the time. As an American, he was imprisoned by the Nazis in 1941 and may hold a negative view about their actions towards him as a result. Also, the fact that he comes from America, a nation that prides itself on freedom of speech, might mean that he found what he saw particularly unpleasant.

Page 55

DESCRIBE

a Mind-map might include for the 'Grumbling or moaning' branch

- Lowest type of opposition.
- Done in the privacy of own homes.

Example:

- People might tell an anti-Nazi joke or complain about the Nazi regime.

Why?

- People too scared to speak publicly because of fear.
- They felt 'safer' in their own homes.

b Reasons might include:

- Terror network (Gestapo, concentration camps, SS, etc.) meant that some were too fearful to speak out or take action.
- Lack of support from other countries (the Beck-Goerdeler group) meant that nothing was done.
- Luck – July Bomb Plot failure.
- Lack of will by general population – many Germans admired Hitler and liked what the Nazis were doing. For example, many teenagers enjoyed the adventures they had in the Hitler Youth; employed people were motivated by the Strength through Joy movement and the work conditions improved by the German Labour Front.

c Answer should include detail about two ways from the following: 'Grumbling or moaning, passive resistance, open opposition, attempts to kill Hitler.

INTERPRETATION ANALYSIS

a The author writes that German newspapers, radio and film were 'stupid and boring'. He thinks that they were not popular with the German people who showed their dislike by choosing to see foreign films and hissing at the German ones.

b As an American, Shirer would stick up for films made in America, in Hollywood. He is used to a culture in which he can express an opinion without any fear and would be both shocked and critical of the tight Nazi controls. It is also his job as a journalist to report in this way.

c It is convincing that people should choose to spend money on films that they will enjoy. So it is convincing that Germans would stay away from boring German-made films. However, to voice criticism of German radio and films was viewed as 'treason' and 'insulting' by the Nazis, so it is less convincing because from 1934 to 1940, it is likely that ordinary Germans would not have criticised Nazi art and media because they feared punishment.

Glossary

A

abdicate: give up the throne of a country

Article 48: part of the Weimar Constitution that gave the President the right to rule in a time of crisis without requiring the support of the Reichstag

avant-garde: new and experimental ideas and methods in art, music, or literature

B

Bauhaus: school of design originating in Weimar Germany, which focused on modern, simple and practical designs

Bundesrat: group made up of German state representatives who supported the Kaiser

C

Chancellor: in Germany, the chief minister, or Prime Minister in the government

coalition: government where two or more political parties combine to rule

communism: political system where all property is owned by the government; people are equal and they are paid by the government according to their needs

concentration camp: camp in which people are held under harsh conditions and without the freedoms of the rest of society

constitution: set of rules by which a country is governed

D

Dawes Plan: agreement allowing for US loans to be given to European countries (especially Germany) in order for them to build factories and roads, and stimulate the economy

democratic republic: system of running a country in which all adults have the right to vote for the government they want

Depression: time during the 1930s when many banks and businesses failed and millions lost their jobs

Der Führer: supreme leader, the title adopted by Adolf Hitler

diktat: nickname given by many Germans to the hated Treaty of Versailles; translated as 'dictated peace'

E

Edelweiss Pirates: rebel youth gang which went camping and sang songs making fun of Hitler; they even physically attacked Hitler Youth groups

Einsatzgruppen: SS mobile death squads responsible for the murder of those thought by the Nazis to be racial or political enemies

Enabling Act: law passed in 1933 that allowed the Nazis to make their own laws without consulting the Reichstag

eugenics: the science of improving a population by controlled breeding

F

Four Year Plan: attempt by the Nazis to increase agricultural and industrial production, regulate imports and exports, and achieve self-sufficiency in the production of raw materials

G

Gestapo: part of the SS and Nazi Germany's secret police force, created by Herman Goering in 1933 and controlled by Heinrich Himmler

ghetto: area where members of a particular racial group are forced (or in some cases choose) to live

H

Holocaust: the mass murder of millions of Jews by the Nazis during the Second World War

hyperinflation: sudden, dramatic rise in prices

I

industrialisation: process by which a country transforms from a mainly agricultural society to one based on manufacturing

K

Kaiser: the German emperor

Kinder, Kirche and *Küche:* 'Children, Church and Cooking'; a slogan used by the Nazis which reflected what women should dedicate their lives to

L

League of Nations: international peace-keeping organisation set up after the First World War; Germany joined in 1926

left-wing: political belief that promotes equality, high taxation for the rich, and the redistribution of wealth

M

master race: elite race of people, to which Hitler believed the Germans belonged

mutiny: rebellion by soldiers or sailors who refuse to take orders

P

propaganda: the systematic spreading of ideas and information in order to influence people's thinking and actions, often through the use of media such as posters, film, radio and newspapers

proportional representation: political system in which the number of politicians for a particular party is in proportion with the number of votes they win

R

Reichstag: the main, elected German parliament

reparations: payments made by Germany to some of the winning nations of the First World War for the damage done by the fighting

right-wing: political belief that promotes traditional or conservative policies

S

Schutzstaffel (SS): originally Hitler's elite personal bodyguards, the SS became one of the main instruments of terror in Nazi Germany

self-sufficient: having a 'closed economy', which meant that the Nazis tried to stop trading with the outside world and rely entirely on its own resources

socialism: system of government which supports democracy and greater government involvement in the economy and society

Spartacus League: group of German communists who wanted a revolution similar to the one that had taken place in Russia in 1917

Stormtroopers (SA): Hitler's brown-shirted supporters who were employed to beat up opponents and guard meetings

Swing Youth: group of young Germans who refused to join the Hitler Youth Organisation

T

Total War: the idea that all Germans, both civilians and soldiers fighting at the fronts, must take an active part in war

W

Weimar Republic: name given to Germany's democratic system between 1913 and 1933

Weltpolitik: literally meaning 'world policy', this was the Kaiser's plan to turn Germany into a global power

White Rose group: anti-Nazi youth group, made up mainly of university students

Y

Young Plan: agreement to reduce reparations, made in 1929 between Germany and the countries they owed money to after the First World War

Topics available from *Oxford AQA GCSE History*

Student Books and Kerboodle Books

Paper One: understanding the modern world

Period Study

Germany 1890–1945 Democracy and Dictatorship
Student Book
978 019 837010 9

Kerboodle Book
978 019 837014 7

America 1920–1973 Opportunity and Inequality
Student Book
978 019 841262 5

Kerboodle Book
978 019 841263 2

Wider World Depth Study

Conflict and Tension: The Inter-War Years 1918–1939
Student Book
978 0 19 837011 6

Kerboodle Book
978 019 837015 4

Conflict and Tension between East and West 1945–1972
Student Book
978 019 841266 3

Kerboodle Book
978 019 841267 0

Conflict and Tension in Asia 1950–1975
Student Book
978 019 841264 9

Kerboodle Book
978 019 841265 6

Conflict and Tension: First World War 1894–1918
Student Book
978 019 842900 5

Kerboodle Book
978 019 842901 2

Paper Two: Shaping the nation

Thematic Study

Thematic Studies c790–Present Day
Student Book
978 019 837013 0

Kerboodle Book
978 019 837017 8

Contents include **all 3 Thematic Study options:** Health, Power, and Migration, Empires and the People

British Depth Study

British Depth Studies c1066–1685
Student Book
978 019 837012 3

Kerboodle Book
978 019 837016 1

Contents include **all 4 British Depth Study options:** Norman, Medieval, Elizabethan, and Restoration England

---

Covering all 16 options

Teacher Handbook

Teacher Handbook
978 019 837018 5

Kerboodle Exam Practice and Revision

Kerboodle Exam Practice and Revision
978 019 837019 2

Revision Guides   RECAP APPLY REVIEW SUCCEED

Germany 1890–1945 Democracy and Dictatorship
Revision Guide: 978 019 842289 1
Kindle edition: 978 019 842290 7

America 1920–1973 Opportunity and Inequality
Revision Guide: 978 019 843282 1
Kindle edition: 978 019 843283 8

Conflict and Tension: The Inter-War Years 1918–1939
Revision Guide: 978 019 842291 4
Kindle edition: 978 019 842292 1

Conflict and Tension between East and West 1945–1972
Revision Guide: 978 019 843288 3
Kindle edition: 978 019 343289 0

Conflict and Tension in Asia 1950–1975
Revision Guide: 978 019 843286 9
Kindle edition: 978 019 843287 6

Britain: Power and the People c1170–Present Day
Revision Guide: 978 019 843290 6
Kindle edition: 978 019 843291 3

Health and the People c1000–Present Day
Revision Guide: 978 019 842295 2
Kindle edition: 978 019 842296 9

Norman England c1066–c1100
Revision Guide: 978 019 843284 5
Kindle edition: 978 019 843285 2

Elizabethan England c1568–1603
Revision Guide: 978 019 842293 8
Kindle edition: 978 019 842294 5

Order online at **www.oxfordsecondary.co.uk/aqa-gcse-history**   OXFORD